A note on the Exceeding the Common Core State Standards series:

We undertook this series of three books (*Get It Done! Writing and Analyzing Informational Texts to Make Things Happen*; *Oh, Yeah?! Putting Argument to Work Both in School and Out*; *So, What's the Story? Teaching Narrative to Understand Ourselves, Others, and the World*) as a collaborative project designed to share our ideas on how to teach the three types of writing addressed by the Common Core State Standards in such a way that students will develop the knowledge they need to do important work both in and out of school. Each of us took the lead in writing one volume and the other two made or suggested a variety of revisions. We are able to work together because we share so much about what we think makes good writing and good teaching, so you'll see many, many similarities across the books, especially in the central principles we use to organize them. But you'll also see some differences in our approaches and in our points of emphasis. To paraphrase Mark Twain, we make this explanation for the reason that without it many readers would suppose that all three authors were trying to talk alike and not succeeding.

oh, Yeah?!

Putting Argument to Work Both in School and Out

Michael W. Smith

Jeffrey D. Wilhelm

James E. Fredricksen

HEINEMANN
Portsmouth, NH

Heinemann
361 Hanover Street
Portsmouth, NH 03801–3912
www.heinemann.com

Offices and agents throughout the world

The authors and publisher wish to thank those who have generously given permission to reprint borrowed material:

Excerpts from *Common Core State Standards* © Copyright 2010. National Governors Association Center for Best Practices and Council of Chief State School Officers. All rights reserved.

A version of "Final Cut" first appeared in *Edge* published by Hampton-Brown. Copyright © by Hampton-Brown. Reprinted by permission of Hampton-Brown and National Geographic Learning, a part of Cengage Learning. All rights reserved.

Library of Congress Cataloging-in-Publication Data
Smith, Michael W.
    Oh, *yeah*?! : putting argument to work both in school and out / Michael W. Smith, Jeffrey D. Wilhelm, James E. Fredricksen.
        p. cm. – (Exceeding the common core state standards)
    Includes bibliographical references and index.
    ISBN-13: 978-0-325-04290-9
    ISBN-10: 0-325-04290-X
    1. Persuasion (Rhetoric)—Study and teaching. 2. Debates and debating—Study and teaching.   I. Wilhelm, Jeffrey D.   II. Fredricksen, James E.   III. Title.

P301.5.P47S63 2012
808'.042071—dc23   2012021743

Editor: Samantha Bennett
Production: Vicki Kasabian
Interior and cover designs: Monica Crigler
Cover photo: Corbis
Typesetter: Valerie Levy / Drawing Board Studios
Manufacturing: Steve Bernier

Printed in the United States of America on acid-free paper
16   15   14   13   VP   3   4   5

To Peter Smagorinsky
Great friend and great model of never giving up
on doing work that makes schools better places for all students

Contents

Acknowledgments

You can see throughout this book the debt of gratitude we owe to so many people. Michael would first like to thank his students Olufemi Fadiyibi, Mary Beth Monahan, and Kristen Turner for allowing him to share their work. Kristen also read and commented on a draft of this book. Her suggestions made it clearer and more user friendly. Michael would also like to thank his colleagues from the University of Chicago who have done so much to shape his thinking on the teaching of writing, especially George Hillocks Jr., Steve Gevinson, the late Larry Johannessen, Betsy Kahn, Carol Lee, Steve Littell, Tom McCann, Peter Smagorinsky, and Carolyn Calhoun Walter. Thanks, too, to his colleagues in the Department of Curriculum, Instruction, and Technology in Education at Temple University's College of Education for making the department such a good place to work. A special thanks to his Department Manager David Devenney whose hard work was largely responsible for Michael's being able to carve out the time he needed to write. Peter Adams, an email colleague from Australia, read early chapters of the book. His thoughtful critique affected what followed. Finally, thanks to Samantha Bennett, our editor, and the whole Heinemann production and marketing teams for their efforts in bringing this book to life. On a personal note: Michael would like to thank the amazing women that fill his life: his wife Karen Flynn, his daughters Catherine and Rachel, and his granddaughter Gabrielle. You give meaning to all that I do.

Jeff thanks Connie Bates for her kindness and support. Gratitude goes to the fellows of the Boise State Writing Project and the members of the CCSS national implementation team, particularly Rachel Bear, Anna Daley, Angie Young, Erika Boas, Cecilia Pattee, Frank Dehoney, and Brandon Bolyard. Thanks too to the National Writing Project for all its leadership and support, particularly Tanya Baker. Thanks, as always, to friends like Brian White and Deb Appleman, who are supportive in so many professional and personal ways. And continuous gratitude to his wife Peggy Jo Wilhelm and daughters Fiona Luray and Jasmine Marie.

Jim thanks Leah Zuidema for her weekly conversations about our teaching and learning. Many thanks also to colleagues across the country, including Anne Whitney, Troy Hicks, Rob Petrone, Les Burns, Jory Brass, Mark Lewis, Mitch Nobis, Beth Harris, and Christine Voreis, for the ongoing personal and professional conversations that sustain him. The hard work and careful insights of the Boise State Writing Project fellows, particularly Rachel Bear, Paula Uriarte, Jessica Westhoff, and Angie Young, have been a real resource. A special note also to colleagues in the English department at Boise State, especially those who offered their insights and asked really smart questions, including Bruce Ballenger, Heidi Estrem, Martin Corliss-Smith, Bruce Robbins, and Tom Hillard. Finally, as always, many thanks to Jim's family and friends, who keep the work in perspective and life fun.

Getting Started

Let's begin with a thought experiment. Think back over the last day or so of your life and identify several arguments that you've participated in. Not shouting matches, but rather occasions in which you staked some kind of claim. When we did, we noticed just how filled with argumentation our lives are. Yesterday, Michael led a discussion at his Collegial Assembly at which he and his colleagues talked about how decision-making power should be distributed in the College of Education, with some arguing that it should reside primarily in departments and others arguing that it should more appropriately reside in the dean's office and in college standing committees. Michael wore a sports jacket to the Assembly, a subtle argument that although semester grades had been submitted, summer hadn't started quite yet. When he got home, he attempted to persuade his college-age daughter that she should get started packing up her apartment and not wait until the last minute. While watching baseball on TV, he wondered just what beer companies are trying to suggest by featuring men who behave so immaturely and thought to himself that those commercials would certainly be more effective if the characters were more appealing. Like most days, he won some, and he lost some.

Jeff began his day by calling several friends and making the case that based on water levels, snow melt, and the weather report, this was the weekend that they should do a float trip down the Owyhee River Canyon near Boise. He then took his wife Peggy to the hematologist, and based on her latest blood counts, all three of them made different proposals for how to proceed with a treatment plan, each of them displaying different valuing of pain, worries about side effects, and the relative importance of the short- and long-term future. Leaving the doctor's office, Jeff and Peggy discussed whether to go out for breakfast or go home and eat. Because it was nearly 9 A.M. and both of them had a lot to do, they decided to go home. Jeff was already dressed for work, which was a subtle argument that he was ready to begin his work day. On the way home, they discussed whether they should support their college-age daughters' claims that they should be allowed to do internships abroad during the summer. Arguments galore, and the day had barely begun.

Jim was on vacation, a trip back to Chicago to see his family. He was lucky enough to get tickets to see the Cubs play the Phillies. To get to Wrigley Field, he took the Metra train into Chicago. Once in the city, he then walked the six blocks to the El, where he took the Red Line to the ballpark. Taking public transportation, rather than driving into and throughout the city, was an intentional claim about the best, most effective, least intrusive way to travel. At the game, Jim sat with his friends—all fans of the Cubs, all wearing blue—an argument to support the home team. During the game, Jim and his friends talked statistics and strategy, making arguments about the lineup, the manager's use of the bullpen, and what trades should be made and when—not unlike many of the arguments heard on sports talk radio or in the sports pages and blogs. No vacation from arguments here.

The purpose of this book is to share our ideas about how to teach the writing of argument so that students will exceed the Common Core State Standards and, in so doing, be prepared for their future lives as students and citizens. This purpose immediately raises two questions: "Why argument?" and "Why the Common Core State Standards?"

Why Argument?

Our anecdotes provide a quick answer to the first query: Arguments abound, both in school and out. In fact, according to Lunsford, Ruszkiewicz, and Walters (2007), argument is endemic in the culture. They title their book *Everything's an Argument* and contend that

> From the clothes you wear to the foods you choose to eat to
> the groups you decide to join—all of these everyday activities
> make nuanced, sometime implicit arguments about who you

are and what you value. Thus an argument can be any text—whether written, spoken or visual—that expresses a point of view. (4)

Argumentation is especially important in a democratic society. Richard Andrews (2009) puts it very nicely:

> Imagine, for a moment, a world without argument. It would either be an authoritarian or tyrannical state, or like the island of Tennyson's lotos-eaters where "All round the coast the languid air did swoon/Breathing like one that hath a weary dream"—a land where intellect and difference are suspended. So, simply to wake up, to be fully conscious, is to be ready for argumentation; for discussion "with edge." (3–4)

We might think that some politicians are not fully conscious and might wish that their talk was somewhat less edgy, but it's hard to deny that argument is and should be at the center of political discourse.

Just as we want our society to be a place where intellect and difference are celebrated, where we think proactively instead of just reactively about problems and how to solve them, where we respond with articulate empathy to others' interests and concerns, so too do we want our classrooms to provide forums for vibrant intellectual exchanges. It is little wonder that schools place such an emphasis on argumentation. Here's Andrews (2009) again:

> [Argument] also refers to the most highly prized type of academic discourse: something that is deemed essential to a thesis, to an article in a research journal, to a dissertation, essay, and to many other kinds of writing within schools and the academy. (1)

Conley (2010) concurs. Through his discussion with college faculty members nationwide, he identified what he calls five key cognitive strategies that are important across disciplines. These strategies are problem formulation, research, interpretation, precision and accuracy, and communication. Communication is the culmination of the other strategies. Conley describes it this way:

> The student constructs well-reasoned arguments or proofs to explain phenomena or issues, uses recognized forms of

reasoning to construct an argument and defend a point of view or conclusion, accepts critiques of or challenges to assertions, and addresses critiques and challenges by providing a logical explanation or refutation or acknowledging the accuracy of the critique or challenge. (34)

In short, successful college students have to be able to employ the cognitive strategies that enable them to craft effective arguments in their chosen disciplines.

If you google "the importance of written argument" you can find plenty of corroboration for Conley's analysis. Here's what the writing center at the University of North Carolina (Writing Center 2010–2012) has to say:

You may be surprised to hear that the word "argument" does not have to be written anywhere in your assignment for it to be an important part of your task. In fact, making an argument— expressing a point of view on a subject and supporting it with evidence—is often the aim of academic writing. Your instructors may assume that you know this and thus may not explain the importance of arguments in class.

Most material you learn in college is or has been debated by someone, somewhere, at some time. Even when the material you read or hear is presented as simple "fact," it may actually be one person's interpretation of a set of information. Instructors may call on you to examine that interpretation and defend it, refute it, or offer some new view of your own. In writing assignments, you will almost always need to do more than just summarize information that you have gathered or regurgitate facts that have been discussed in class. You will need to develop a point of view on or interpretation of that material and provide evidence for your position.

And here's the conclusion of Dartmouth's writing program's discussion (Gocsik 2005) of what makes an academic paper:

Academic writing should present the reader with an informed argument. To construct an informed argument, you must first try to sort out what you *know* about a subject from what you *think* about a subject. Or, to put it another way, you will want to consider what *is known* about a subject and then to determine what *you* think about it. If your paper fails to inform, or if it fails to argue, then it will fail to meet the expectations of the academic reader.

But it's not just writing centers. After noting that reader skepticism is likely to co-vary with the importance of the policy about which one is writing, an instructor (Halstead n.d.) in the Harvard School of Public Health writes

> To meet this challenge, authors must first critically evaluate
> all the relevant evidence and then present the entire story as a
> *logical sequence* of *reasons* and *evidence* in support of a conclusion
> or *claim*. In other words, writers need to frame their work as
> *critical arguments*.

And it's not just teachers at our nation's most elite universities who write about the importance of argument. Here's what an instructor of English at Delaware Technical and Community College (Reid n.d.) says about writing proposals:

> The general purpose of any proposal is to persuade the readers
> to do something, whether it is to persuade a potential customer
> to purchase goods and / or services, or to persuade your
> employer to fund a project or to implement a program that you
> would like to launch.

Proposals are a crucial genre of technical writing, she explains, and are, in essence, arguments.

It's little wonder that the Common Core State Standards (CCSS) place such an emphasis on writing argument. Indeed, the authors of the CCSS, the Council of Chief State School Officers (CCSSO) and the National Governors Association Center for Best Practices, explain

> [T]he Standards put particular emphasis on students' ability to
> write sound arguments on substantive topics and issues, as this
> ability is critical to college and career readiness. English and
> education professor Gerald Graff (2003) writes that "argument
> literacy" is fundamental to being educated. The university
> is largely an "argument culture," Graff contends; therefore,
> K–12 schools should "teach the conflicts" so that students are

adept at understanding and engaging in argument (both oral and written) when they enter college. He claims that because argument is not standard in most school curricula, only 20 percent of those who enter college are prepared in this respect. Theorist and critic Neil Postman (1997) calls argument the soul of an education because argument forces a writer to evaluate the strengths and weaknesses of multiple perspectives. When teachers ask students to consider two or more perspectives on a topic or issue, something far beyond surface knowledge is required: students must think critically and deeply, assess the validity of their own thinking, and anticipate counterclaims in opposition to their own assertions. (26)

It seems clear that there is a strong consensus on the importance of being able to compose effective arguments. But we also know that the CCSS have not been universally embraced. Before we go on, therefore, we think it's important for us to address why we will be using the CCSS as a touchstone throughout this book as well as throughout its companion books on teaching exposition and narrative.

Why the Common Core State Standards?

One reason that we'll be referring to the CCSS is that 45 states have adopted them at the time of this writing and that other states are likely to do so in the near future. It's far easier for us to write about a single set of standards than to do a content analysis of distinct standards from all 50 states and to adjust our discussion on the basis of that analysis.

But it's not just that the CCSS reduce the rhetorical complexity of trying to reach a national audience. We admire the goal of "ensur[ing] that all students are college and career ready in literacy no later than the end of high school." We agree that some state standards were not sufficiently rigorous to guarantee that readiness and applaud the fact that when compared to state standards the CCSS would "shift content . . . toward higher levels of cognitive demand" (106) according to a recent analysis (Porter, McMaken, Hwang, Yang 2011).

At the same time, we worry along with Ravitch (2010) that any standards movement is susceptible to getting "hijacked" by testing and that likewise curricula are hijacked by test preparation. Moore (2011) raises the concern that the move to the CCSS is motivated by commercial interests rather than educational ones. And Beach (2011) points out that the CCSS may be understood and implemented in very different ways by different teachers, suggesting that the CCSS' intention could be undercut by teachers reducing the teaching of writing to some kind of formula.

Yet we remained convinced by Langer (2001) that across communities of varying socioeconomic status instruction directed to improving student performance on standards-based assessments can be very powerful instruction indeed. Here's how she puts it:

> In the most successful schools, there was always a belief in students' abilities to be able and enthusiastic learners; they believed all students can learn and that they, as teachers, could make a difference. They therefore took on the hard job of providing rich and challenging instructional contexts in which important discussions about English, language, literature, and writing in all its forms could take place, while using both the direct instruction and contextualized experiences their students needed for skills and knowledge development. Weaving a web of integrated and interconnected experiences, they ensured that their students would develop the pervasive as well as internalized learning of knowledge, skills, and strategies to use on their own as more mature and more highly literate individuals at school, as well as at home and in their future work. (876)

Let's take it even a step farther: We believe that instruction directed toward improving student performance on standards-based assessments *must* be the most powerful and engaging instruction we can possibly offer. Like Langer, we think that means providing enough clear and compelling instruction and sufficient practice so that all students can succeed. Like Langer, we think that means creating contexts that make it clear to students why what we're teaching matters in the here and now, as well as in the future. Like Langer, we think that means providing the opportunity and support for students to transfer what they have learned to new work they will do, both in and out of school. In short, we see the CCSS as a powerful lever we can use in promoting progressive practice.

So What Do the CCSS Say About Argument?

As we have argued, the CCSS are absolutely clear about the centrality of argument to their conception of teaching the English language arts and in teaching and learning in the disciplines. Here's the first "key point" the CCSS' website makes about writing: "The ability to write logical arguments based on substantive claims, sound reasoning, and relevant evidence is a cornerstone of the writing standards, with opinion writing—a basic form of argument—extending down into the earliest grades."

Here's what the CCSS say that sixth graders should be able to do:

1. Write arguments to support claims with clear reasons and relevant evidence.

    a. Introduce claim(s) and organize the reasons and evidence clearly.

    b. Support claim(s) with clear reasons and relevant evidence, using credible sources and demonstrating an understanding of the topic or text.

    c. Use words, phrases, and clauses to clarify the relationships among claim(s) and reasons.

    d. Establish and maintain a formal style.

    e. Provide a concluding statement or section that follows from the argument presented.

The CCSS ratchet up the expectations grade by grade, culminating with these expectations for eleventh and twelfth graders:

1. Write arguments to support claims in an analysis of substantive topics or texts, using valid reasoning and relevant and sufficient evidence.

    a. Introduce precise, knowledgeable claim(s), establish the significance of the claim(s), distinguish the claim(s) from alternate or opposing claims, and create an organization that logically sequences claim(s), counterclaims, reasons, and evidence.

    b. Develop claim(s) and counterclaims fairly and thoroughly, supplying the most relevant evidence for each while pointing out the strengths and limitations of both in a manner that anticipates the audience's knowledge level, concerns, values, and possible biases.

   c. Use words, phrases, and clauses as well as varied syntax to link the major sections of the text, create cohesion, and clarify the relationships between claim(s) and reasons, between reasons and evidence, and between claim(s) and counterclaims.

   d. Establish and maintain a formal style and objective tone while attending to the norms and conventions of the discipline in which they are writing.

   e. Provide a concluding statement or section that follows from and supports the argument presented.

According to the CCSS, arguments must be built around clear claims and by the eleventh and twelfth grade those claims must be significant ones that take a distinct position amid competing claims. They must also be effectively supported and organized. By eleventh and twelfth grade the idea of support includes responding to counterclaims and includes constructing the argument with an awareness of the audience's knowledge and biases. The argument must be cohesive. That is, the writer must be able to articulate the relationship among the sentences and sections of the argument. The concluding statement (in sixth grade) or the more developed conclusion (in eleventh and twelfth grade) needs to follow from and support the argument. Finally, the argument must employ appropriate and varied syntactic structures and must be written in an appropriately formal tone. By eleventh and twelfth grade the argument must also follow the norms and convention of the discipline in which it's written. We'll be talking much more about instruction designed to achieve each of these standards. We think it's worth noting, however, that all of the CCSS standards, except for the ones on appropriateness, are related to the structure of the argument. In Chapter 2, we'll provide a more extensive discussion of just what the structure of an effective argument looks like.

Implications for Planning and Practice

Before we do so, we'd like to highlight two important implications of this chapter—two ways to get you started on your work with the CCSS. The first may seem obvious, but we're afraid it's not: Spend enough time with the CCSS to really get to know them and think hard about the theories of writing that undergird them. For example, the

CCSS suggest a belief that different kinds of writing (argumentative, informational, and narrative) work differently. Michael and his friend Peter Smagorinsky (1992) labeled this position the task-specific position and contrast it to the position that holds that writers work in essentially the same way regardless of the kind of writing they are doing—what they term the general knowledge position. Talking with colleagues about what these modes of writing have in common and what they don't will help you start thinking about how much time you'll need to devote specifically to argument.

We also suggest examining the principles of sequence of the CCSS. When should students begin writing arguments? Why? What principles of sequence do the CCSS invoke and how do they match up to your curriculum? One of the disturbing findings of George Hillocks' book *The Testing Trap* (2002) is that few teachers undertook any kind of systematic analysis of the tests designed to assess achievement of state standards. We hope that the CCSS and the assessments that measure them will receive far more thoughtful and systematic consideration.

The second is to begin collecting arguments of various sorts, both academic arguments and those that are made outside of school. The ubiquity of arguments should make this a relatively easy thing to do. We suggest looking both for arguments that you find compelling, ones that can serve as mentor texts, and those that don't work so well, ones you might call upon your students to critique or revise. This collection will serve you well when you're teaching the structure of arguments, the topic of our next chapter.

CHAPTER 2

Thinking About the Structure of an Effective Argument

The 2007 National Assessment of Educational Progress (NAEP) report on writing performance contains some good news. The average writing scores and the percentages of students performing at or above Basic were higher in 2007—the last year for which we have data at the time of this writing—than they were in both 1998 and 2002 at both the eighth and twelfth grades. The African American/European American achievement gap narrowed at grade 8 compared to 1998 and 2002, though it showed no significant change at grade 12. But amid that good news is this sobering finding: Almost three-quarters of twelfth-grade students scored below proficient on their writing sample.

NAEP doesn't disaggregate scores based on genre, but it's worth noting that 40 percent of the writing prompts called for persuasive writing, so it seems safe to say that NAEP establishes that most adolescents are not proficient at argumentation. Which leads us to wonder whether the folks at NAEP have ever talked to an adolescent? Our students and our own kids, we've found, are exceptionally accomplished arguers. Our lives would be much easier were that not the case!

This perplexing discrepancy suggests to us that it's useful to think about the nature of oral argumentation to understand why it is that young people, who so effectively state their cases in conversation, have trouble doing so when they write. If we can build bridges between oral and written argumentation, our students will surely benefit.

Turning to Toulmin

As you recall from the last chapter, the CCSS state that students beginning in sixth grade should be able to write well-organized and well-supported arguments to establish clear and significant claims. But the CCSS don't specify what they mean by "significant" claims, nor what they mean by supporting an argument effectively. Like a growing number of teachers of writing, we've found that the work of Stephen Toulmin has been an invaluable aid in that specification. Toulmin's (1958) analysis of everyday arguments has been especially compelling to us because it is so well suited to capitalize on students' oral abilities.

Claims

Toulmin's analysis of argument is based on a consideration of the kind of arguments people have in real life as opposed to the formal logic used to ascertain universal principles. Think about an oral argument you have had recently. It almost certainly began with a statement with which your conversational partner disagreed. Toulmin calls these statements *claims*. All three of us are sports fans, and one of the reasons we love sports is because of the conversations they engender. Jeff's a college basketball fan, so he might say, "College basketball is a much better game than pro basketball." Michael, a pro fan, would disagree. Jim's a Cubs fan while Michael's a White Sox fan; plenty of grist for argument there. And Jeff roots for the Indians *and* the Red Sox, while Jim and Michael would argue that rooting for two teams in the same league suggests a severe character deficiency.

But the stakes of arguments in other domains are much higher. The four stories above the fold on the front page of the *New York Times* on the date this section was drafted (May 27, 2011) are all centered on arguments. Headline: "Illegal Workers: Court Upholds Faulting Hirers." The story centers on the claim made by Arizona that states ought to be able to supplement federal efforts to discourage the hiring of illegal workers. Headline: "Study Questions Treatment Used in Heart Disease." The story reports the results of a study whose central claim is that therapies that try to raise good cholesterol along with reducing bad cholesterol are no more effective than therapies that only work to reduce bad cholesterol. Headline: "China's Farming Pursuits Make Brazil Uneasy." The story reports on the differing views of whether the former president of Brazil was wise to pursue a strategic partnership with China. Headline: "Serb Ex-General Accused of Massacre Is Captured." The story reports on competing opinions on the capture and the impact it will have on Serbia's relationship with the rest of the world, particularly the European Union.

Whether you consider the quotidian examples of our sports debates or the much more important arguments that earn a spot on the front page, it seems clear that generative claims have two primary features: They are both debatable and defensible. If Jeff were to argue that college basketball is a very popular sport on some American campuses, Michael wouldn't take up the argument. The popularity of basketball on some campuses is clear. If Jeff were to argue that college players are superior to pro players, instead of taking up the argument, Michael would dismiss it as obviously false. If the claim that states ought to be able to supplement federal efforts to discouraging the hiring of illegal workers weren't controversial, it wouldn't need to be litigated. If it weren't defensible, it wouldn't have resulted in a split decision.

Data

In conversation, once you've made a controversial claim, you're likely to be asked something like the following: "What makes you say so?" or "What do you have to go on?" The answer to that question is what Toulmin (1958) calls the grounds, or *data*, for the argument. Think back to one of the arguments we gave as an example: Cubs versus White Sox. If Jim made the argument that the Cubs were better than the White Sox at the time of this writing, Michael would ask, "What makes you say so?" If Jim said, "Because the Cubs have better pitching," Michael would say, "What makes you say so?" Jim's response to Michael's question, then, isn't data for his argument. Rather it's another claim. In contrast to claims, data have to provide a safe starting point for the argument, something that the audience will either have to accept or be willing to stipulate to. If Jim said something like "The Cubs have a more experienced closer," Michael would have to agree (the White Sox closer in 2011 was a rookie) and the argument could continue. What makes something data is that it is evidence that is beyond dispute. It answers the question "What makes you say so?" and provides something to go on since both parties, at least initially, can agree on it.

Warrants and Backing

However, as Toulmin (1958) points out, simply providing data doesn't clinch the argument. Once someone provides data, a conversational partner will ask, "So what?" That is, "Why do those data matter?" Or "What allows you to move from those data to that claim?" The answer to the "So what?" question is what Toulmin calls a *warrant*.

In our judgment, warrants are the least understood element of Toulmin's model, so we'll spend some time with them. Let's go back to the Cubs versus White Sox example. Although Michael has to grant that the Cubs have a more experienced closer, doing so only matters if Jim can provide a connection from his data to his claim, a general rule along the lines of "Having an experienced closer is an essential element of a good team." Let's take another everyday example. Michael and his wife Karen have an ongoing argument about who's the greater actor, Johnny Depp or Clint Eastwood. Karen maintains that Johnny Depp is better because he plays such different roles, from the lawless pirate Jack Sparrow to the very proper Victorian author J. M. Barrie. Michael responds that Clint Eastwood is better because he was one of the top-ten money-making stars twenty-one different years. The data are clear. They can be verified. Karen and Michael's argument hinges on competing warrants. For Karen, it's "Versatility is the *sine qua non* of great actors." For Michael, it's "Longevity is the surest indication of greatness."

As teachers, many of the arguments we have to consider also depend on warrants. Let's think, for example, about the controversy over whether to teach *The Adventures of Huckleberry Finn*. One side might argue, "It contains words that may offend some readers." The other might say, "It's one of the most influential books in American literary history." Both statements seem to us to pass muster as safe starting points. But neither is enough. The first piece of data requires a warrant like "Teachers should not teach books that some students or their parents find offensive." The second requires something like "Teachers ought to teach books that have proven to be important historically."

Because warrants are general rules, they resemble the major premise of an Aristotelian syllogism, but they differ in important ways. Aristotle illustrates syllogistic reasoning with this famous example:

All men are mortal.

Socrates is a man.

Socrates is mortal.

But Toulmin rightly points out that in the real world, people don't argue in domains in which there is such certainty. If all men are mortal, of course Socrates is mortal. No one would ever argue otherwise. Keith and Beard (2008) provide a nice explanation of the difference between the major premise of a syllogism and a warrant:

> In a sense, Toulmin is subtly moving ninety degrees from the classical tradition of logic. In classical logic, the term Aristotle uses to describe the character of logical inference in the syllogism, *anagkhaios,* is usually translated as *necessary,* but it might also be rendered as *constrained* or *compulsory*; in a valid syllogism the reasoner "needs to" draw the conclusion. In contrast, in a Toulmin argument, she is *allowed* to draw the conclusion. (22)

Because warrants in the real world are not compulsory, they themselves may have to be supported. Consider the public policy debate about reducing the government's funding of Medicaid. The data are unarguable. Doing so would save money but would leave American citizens unprotected, especially those already most at risk. The warrants are the heart of the argument. The conservative position depends on the warrant that reducing the deficit is the government's highest priority. The liberal position depends on the warrant that one of the government's primary responsibilities is protecting its most vulnerable citizens. The argument seems to us to be irreconcilable because of the different general principles. For either side to be effective it would have to convince its audience of the justness of its warrant by providing support for the warrant, what Toulmin (1958) calls *backing*. Very often political parties seek to do so by citing historical examples of one sort or another about the central purpose of government, or by citing the founders or a popular politician of a previous era.

Rebuttals, Qualifiers, and Responses

Because Toulmin (1958) recognizes that most arguments are unlikely to be absolutely convincing, he has to add *rebuttals* to his model. Rebuttals suggest an awareness of potential audience objections. Qualifiers reflect an awareness of possible rebuttals by indicating the conditions under which the claim remains valid. Returning to the baseball example, Jim might say to Michael, "As long as the Cubs' experienced closer remains healthy, the Cubs are the better team." Let's look at the *Huck Finn* example again. A teacher in the *Huck Finn* discussion might say, "I understand that some readers might find *Huck Finn* offensive, but this group of juniors is mature enough to be able to talk about it," indicating that he or she doesn't think that *Huck Finn* should be taught to all groups of juniors.

Although Toulmin himself doesn't write about alternatives to qualifiers, we've found it useful to add the notion of *response* to Toulmin's model. A response works to overcome the objections offered in a rebuttal. So if we return to the baseball example yet again, after presenting his case Michael might say something like "I know the White Sox and the Cubs have virtually the same record, but the White Sox play in a much better league" in an attempt to preempt a response Jim is likely to make before Jim has had a chance to make it.

A summary of Toulmin's model and a graphic representation appear in Figures 2.1 and 2.2. We've filled out the graphic representation with one of our examples (in italics) to illustrate its use.

Before we move on, a note, an aside, and a quick discussion of the next steps you might want to take. The note: What we have summarized here are structural features that are true across contexts, what Toulmin calls *field-invariant elements*. As we'll explore in greater detail in Chapter 3, different argumentative situations have field-dependent aspects as well. However, the shared elements of argument give us a powerful starting point for helping our students develop their abilities in this very crucial arena.

The aside: We recognize that some teachers make a distinction between argument and persuasion. Lunsford, Ruszkiewicz, and Walter (2006) characterize the distinction as follows: "In this view, the point of *argument* is to discover some version of the truth" while "the aim of *persuasion* is to change a point of view

Figure 2.1 A Summary of Toulmin's Model

> *Claim:* The starting point for an argument. Good claims must be both defensible and controversial.
>
> *Data:* Answer the question, "What makes you say so?" or "What do you have to go on?" For an argument to go forward the audience has to at least provisionally accept the data. Data have to provide a safe starting point.
>
> *Warrant:* Answers the question, "So what?" or "What allows you to move from those grounds to that claim?" A warrant is almost always some kind of general principle. Usually warrants have to be supported with *backing*.
>
> *Rebuttal:* What someone who disagrees with any portion of the argument might say. Rebuttals can be addressed by adding a *qualifier* to the claim or by offering a *response* to it.

Figure 2.2

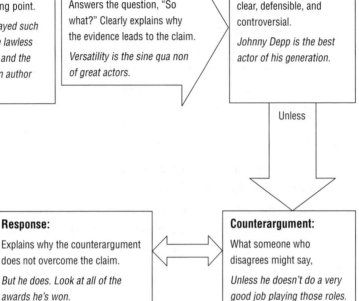

or to move others from conviction to action" (8). That is, some see arguments as appealing to reason while persuasion seeks to change a point of view by any means necessary. We agree with Lunsford and her colleagues that in practice this distinction is difficult to sustain, especially in the public policy and academic arenas that we care so much about. In both arenas we want our students to convince their audiences of the validity of their point of view. We don't want our students to persuade through propaganda and we think that helping them understand how to craft arguments will help them recognize when others are making use of propaganda.

Our emphasis on argumentation is not meant to suggest that convincing others is merely an intellectual exercise. As you will see in the chapters that follow, we believe that emotionally charged narratives and visuals can be compelling data depending on the claim. In short, we don't think the distinction between argument and persuasion is especially useful, so we won't be making that distinction.

Implications for Planning and Practice

If we've convinced you that Toulmin's conception of the structure of arguments is both sensible and easy to use, you should probably spend some time becoming more familiar with it. You might want to take a look at Toulmin, Rieke, and Janik's *An Introduction to Reasoning* (1984), as you may find it more easily accessible than Toulmin's foundational philosophical work. But we think it's even more important to begin using his model to think about the arguments you see and hear around you, the kind of arguments we suggested last chapter that you begin collecting.

As we're doing our final revision of this chapter, it's May 2012. It's primary season in the election cycle, the movie awards season has come and gone, and many publications have released their lists of the year's best movies, and this year's *American Idol* decision is right around the corner. All are fertile ground for finding arguments that you can analyze using Toulmin's framework.

Without further ado, let's move to our next chapter in which we'll introduce you to two heuristics that will help you bring the theoretical work we've done in this chapter into effective practice.

CHAPTER 3

Five Kinds of Knowledge,
Five Kinds of Composing

The Foundations of Our Practice

Thus far we've made an argument for the importance of teaching argument and have considered the elements of a well-reasoned argument. But we haven't addressed what our students need to know to be able to produce those elements as they craft an effective argument. George Hillocks (1986b, 1995) has helped us think about this crucially important question. But before we explain what we learned from George, a story from each of us.

Michael is a pretty good tennis player. He coached when he was in high school and has been playing for coming on 50 years. (Yikes!) This past indoor season, he had terrible trouble with his serve, usually the strongest part of his game. He just couldn't get the toss right and as a consequence his whole form broke down, leading to far too many double-faults. His playing partners would often say something like, "Just get it in," but truth be told, that didn't do any good. That's what he was trying to do! So Michael had to scour his memory for what he had learned from coaches, pros, and instructional books and then hit the courts to apply what he remembered. The toss isn't there yet, but it's getting better.

As we write this, Jeff is getting ready to kayak down the Grand Canyon. It's been a big water year and the release on the river will be 24,000 cfs (cubic feet per second). Yow! That is going to make for some big waves and river features. So Jeff decided to try using a bigger boat. But despite years of rolling a kayak in all kinds of conditions, he couldn't confidently nail the roll with this bigger boat. He knew all the steps. He could recite them to himself as he tried to roll. But his rolls were wobbly and not the kind you want to have when you are in big water or in a big jam. He knew what to do but had lost the capacity to do it with confidence and expertise. It's now two weeks before his trip and he is back in his old boat (needless to say!).

Jim's been taking piano lessons for about a year with the goal of not only being able to play but eventually of being able to improvise. With that goal in mind, Jim's teacher has been working with him not only on particular pieces he practices but also on the theory behind what he's playing. For instance, he's developing a working understanding of chords, of how to transpose, and of how to build the first, fourth, and fifth steps. But he's not yet able to sit in with his friends as they jam; his fingers just don't do what his head knows.

The Inquiry Square: The Importance of Procedural Knowledge

Our stories may not seem momentous, but they make an important point, one that we have to keep reminding ourselves of: *Knowing* what you're supposed to do doesn't mean that you're *able* to do it. You may need instruction, and once you get that instruction, you have to practice and then practice some more. And even if you think you've mastered something, small changes in the task or situation can mean you have to learn more so you can adjust to the new demands.

The long career of George Hillocks, a hero to all three of us, has provided testimony to this powerful and simple truth. He has made this argument many times and in many ways, but one of his first and clearest formulations came in a chapter he wrote in 1986. In that chapter Hillocks (1986b) argues that writers employ four kinds of knowledge. (As you'll see, he later added a fifth kind of knowledge to the equation.) He starts with a distinction long made in cognitive psychology: the difference between declarative and procedural knowledge. *Declarative knowledge* is knowledge of *what*, the kind of knowledge that can be spoken. Knowing that effective arguments need to be supported with data, or that commas follow introductory adverbial clauses is declarative knowledge. *Procedural knowledge*, on the other hand, is knowledge of *how*, a kind of knowledge that has to be performed. Being able to select the best pieces of evidence from a text requires procedural knowledge, as does the ability to compose complex sentences. Hillocks argues further that writers must have knowledge of *substance*, that is, they must know about what they're writing about and knowledge of *form*, that is, they must know the formal features of the kind of text they are trying to produce.

If you put it all together, you have a two-by-two matrix that we term the *inquiry square*. Figure 3.1 displays this matrix. According to Hillocks, all writers must have four kinds of knowledge if they are going to write effectively: declarative knowledge of form, declarative knowledge of substance, procedural knowledge of form, and procedural knowledge of substance.

Let's examine each of them in turn as they relate specifically to writing arguments of one sort or another.

Figure 3.1   Four Kinds of Knowledge

	Declarative	Procedural
Form		
Substance		

Declarative Knowledge of Form

Declarative knowledge of form means knowing the formal characteristics of the writing one intends to produce. Conventional wisdom has it that writers need declarative knowledge of form at the sentence level, for example, knowing that a complete sentence contains a subject and a predicate, though decades of research on the teaching of grammar has challenged this wisdom. (See Smith, Cheville, and Hillocks 2006 for a recent review.) What is unquestioned is that writers need declarative knowledge of form at the genre level. Declarative knowledge of form at the genre level includes knowing that APA-style research reports are typically divided into five sections; that letters to the editor of the *New York Times* cannot exceed 150 words; that media reviews typically rate what's reviewed on a 1–4 or –5 star basis; and so on.

Declarative knowledge of form is, we think, the kind of knowledge privileged in many English classes. Instruction in traditional school grammar seeks to develop declarative knowledge of form. So too does the study of models. So too does the use of rubrics that detail just what it is student writers are expected to do on a given assignment. But as the inquiry square makes clear, this knowledge alone is not enough.

Declarative Knowledge of Substance

Declarative knowledge of substance means knowing the factual or content knowledge that will be included in an argument. For example, if a writer is arguing that *Romeo and Juliet* is the appropriate Shakespeare play to teach to ninth graders, declarative knowledge of substance would include knowing, among other things, the ages of the title characters, the centrality of family conflict to the play, and so on. If a writer is arguing in favor of smoking prohibitions, declarative knowledge of substance would mean knowing what research says about the effect of second-hand smoke. If a writer is arguing the relative merits of two SUVs, declarative knowledge of substance would include knowing the EPA fuel estimates, resale value, seating and storage capacities, and so on.

An emphasis on declarative knowledge of substance, in our view, dominates most literature-based curricula and virtually all of the writing instruction students tend to receive in the disciplines. The idea seems to be that if students understand the literary text about which they have been asked to write, or the historical event they just studied, or the experiment they just performed, or the problem they just solved, then they can write about it. Our jobs would be much easier were this the case. But anyone who has read a set of papers on a literary text can tell you it is not.

Procedural Knowledge of Form

Procedural knowledge, on the other hand, is knowledge of how to put declarative knowledge into practice. For example, procedural knowledge of form on the sentence level means being able to produce complete and correct sentences, being able to use parallel constructions for clarity and rhetorical appeal, and so on. Procedural knowledge of form at the genre level depends on the kind of argument one is producing. For writers of research reports it means, among other things, being able to describe and justify the research methods one used clearly. For writers of letters to the editor of the *New York Times* it means being able to succinctly summarize the argument of the piece to which they are responding. For writers of reviews it means being able to make definitive judgments of quality.

An emphasis on procedural knowledge of form is much less common than an emphasis on either kind of declarative knowledge. At the sentence level, this kind of instruction would include cued sentence combining that targets syntactic structure writers of argument employ (e.g., although proponents of this policy argue *X*, research/experience demonstrates *Y*; see Smith and Wilhelm 2007 for more examples). At the text level it would include extended practice producing (and not just identifying) target structures.

Procedural Knowledge of Substance

Procedural knowledge of substance means knowing how to generate the substance of a text. Writers of research reports have to be able to collect compelling data. Writers of letters to the editor often have to be able to identify flaws in argument of the editorial or story they are critiquing. Writers of reviews have to be able to select the best possible illustrations to support their judgments.

Developing procedural knowledge of substance, that is, teaching kids how to get the stuff about which they will write, is certainly the least emphasized kind of knowledge in writing classrooms. Hillocks (1986a, 1995) calls the focus on procedural knowledge of substance *inquiry* and his research establishes that instruction that focuses on inquiry is the most powerful kind of composition instruction that teachers can provide.

The *Writing Next* (Graham and Perrine 2007) report, a more recent meta-analysis, makes a similar claim, finding that the most powerful kind of writing instruction involves "explicitly and systematically teaching steps necessary for planning, revising, and/or editing text" (15), though it should be noted that this conclusion does not clearly separate an emphasis on procedural knowledge of form and substance.

Both meta-analyses jibe with a recent conceptual review (Andrews, Torgerson, Low, and McGuinn 2009) of successful practice that examined only approaches to teaching argument. Successful practice in the studies reviewed was characterized by a focus on procedural knowledge through providing plenty of opportunities for students to plan, revise, and edit their work; through helping them learn how to set appropriate goals; through providing cognitive reasoning training; and through dialoging with peers. The take-away: All four kinds of knowledge are key, but traditional instruction does a pretty good job developing declarative knowledge. Crucially important procedural knowledge, unfortunately, is too often neglected. As teachers we have to concentrate on the how.

Hillocks' taxonomy makes what we feel are extremely useful distinctions, but like all taxonomies, in articulating those distinctions it blurs relationships. Before we move on, we want to stress that the development of declarative knowledge and procedural knowledge are intimately related. That is, declarative knowledge does not exist prior to procedural knowledge. In fact, according to Vygotsky, "The formation of concepts occurs whenever the adolescent is faced with the task of resolving some problem" (1987, 164). The adolescent's activity is key. Procedural engagement gives rise to declarative understandings.

Moreover, declarative knowledge can't be engendered through a teacher's declarations, an irony that we all need to keep in mind. Here's Vygotsky again:

> No less than experimental research, pedagogical experience demonstrates that direct instruction in concepts is impossible. It is pedagogically fruitless. The teacher who attempts to use this approach achieves nothing but a mindless learning of words. . . . This mode of instruction is the basic defect of the purely scholastic verbal modes of teaching which have been universally condemned. It substitutes the learning of dead and empty verbal schemes for the mastery of living knowledge. (170)

Beyond the Inquiry Square:
The Importance of Context

Living knowledge is messier than verbal schemes, in large measure because it's always situated in a human context. As composition studies has taken a social turn, compositionists, George Hillocks among them, have thought carefully about the extent to which writing is dependent on context. Hillocks makes the importance of context clear in his articulation of a model of the composing process (1995). He draws on his longtime colleague Bernie McCabe (Hillocks, McCabe, and McCampbell 1971) to argue that all writing is situated in both an immediate situation and a wider environment. The immediate situation includes such things as the writer's relationship with his or her immediate audience, especially in terms of the purpose the writer is pursuing. For example, as full professors with tenure Jeff and Michael would not have to be as careful in how they phrased an objection to a department policy as would Jim, an assistant professor without tenure. Misreading the immediate situation, that is, the knowledge and predispositions of the immediate audience, the power relationships that exist among the participants, and so on, can have dire consequence. But the immediate situation is only one element of the context, for the immediate situation is always nested in a wider environment, "namely that of the culture (and possibly cultures) and its institutions" (Hillocks 1995, 85). Let's take another illustration from our work lives. Each of us speak both to audiences who are trained in education and who are trained in English. If we want to establish our theoretical credentials to an audience of educators, we're likely to turn, as we just did, to psychologists like Vygotsky. If we want to do the same for an audience of a university's department of English, we'd be apt to refer to literary theorists like Mikhail Bakhtin or Kenneth Burke. Another quick illustration: Michael has written with Peter Rabinowitz, a literary theorist. On one occasion they scheduled a phone call to get their planning started. Michael wanted to make sure they had the same main points in mind. Peter wanted to make sure they agreed on the central metaphor. Their disciplinary difference resulted in very different approaches to planning. In short, in order to be an effective composer of arguments, one must also be aware of the differing demands and expectations of disciplines, subcultures, institutions, and so on.

Indeed, Toulmin (1958) himself makes the importance of context clear. He notes that his analysis has to take up the question of

> What things about the forms and merits of our arguments are field-invariant and what things about them are field-dependent. What things about the modes in which we assess arguments, the standards by reference to which we assess them and the manner in which we qualify our conclusions to them, are the same regardless of field (field-invariant) and which of them vary as we move from arguments in one field to arguments in another (field-dependent)? (14–15)

In fact, in the concluding section of *An Introduction to Reasoning* (1979), Toulmin and his colleagues consider "special fields of reasoning" and examine legal reasoning, argumentation in science, arguing about the arts, reasoning about management, and ethical reasoning in separate sections. They found that in different fields, different things count as claims worth arguing, data worth citing, and so on.

The importance of both the immediate and wider context means that we have to amend the diagram we presented in Figure 3.1 and replace it with Figure 3.2.

The recognition that both the immediate situation and the wider environment affect how and what one writes seems to us to be crucially important. And it seems very much in line with the CCSS. According to the standards document, students who are college and career ready in reading, writing, speaking, listening, and language

> adapt their communication in relation to audience, task, purpose, and discipline. They set and adjust purpose for reading, writing, speaking, listening, and language use as warranted by the task. They appreciate nuances, such as how the composition of an audience should affect tone when speaking and how the connotations of words affect meaning. They also know that different disciplines call for different types of evidence (e.g., documentary evidence in history, experimental evidence in science). (7)

➤ *CCSS connection*

In short, the CCSS require that students are sensitive to both the micro and macro dimensions of the writing context.

Figure 3.2

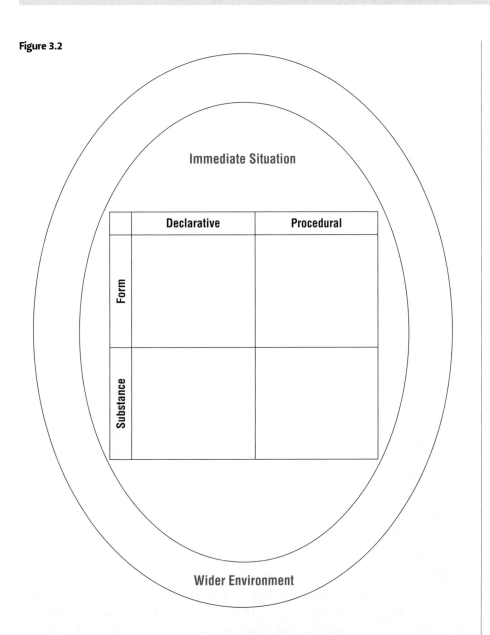

The importance of context means that our instruction has to help students understand what can be transferred and what can't. It means that our colleagues in disciplines other than English are not doing us a favor when they teach scientific or historical or mathematical writing. Rather, the writing they are teaching is at the very heart of their own disciplines.

A Note on Reading

Although our emphasis in this book is on composing arguments, we see composing and consuming arguments as inextricably related. That is, the five kinds of knowledge we identified are just as crucial for readers as they are for writers. If students know the formal features of sound arguments (declarative knowledge of form), then they will be better able to recognize when arguments are missing warrants or proceeding from questionable data (procedural knowledge of form). If we help them gain sufficient knowledge in a domain (declarative knowledge of substance), they'll be able to recognize what new contributions a text makes (procedural knowledge of substance). If we ask them to read widely to get background information and to probe deeply to evaluate whether or not to use a text in their own writing for particular audiences and purposes, they'll see that context matters both to readers and to writers.

Five Kinds of Composing

As our discussion of the five kinds of knowledge critical to composing might suggest, we think taxonomies can have a useful heuristic value for us as teachers. Identifying the five kinds of knowledge helps us make sure that we are working to develop all of them. Our belief in the potential heuristic value of taxonomies means our interest was piqued when we encountered John Collins' delineation of five types of writing (see www.collinsed.com/cwp.htm). But while we admire the impulse behind his project, we found our thinking differing from his in a number of significant ways, so we'll be presenting our own list. But first we want to emphasize why we'll be talking about five kinds of composing instead of five kinds of writing.

As we noted earlier in this chapter, George Hillocks has been an important influence on us. George's work (e.g., 1986a, 1995, 2011) challenges the principle that kids can learn to write only by writing, a principle that seems to us to be too often taken for granted. We wholeheartedly agree that kids can't learn to write by watching someone else write or by listening to someone else talk about writing. In fact, we think that the principle derives in large measure from the recognition that kids have to be actively engaged in their learning.

What Hillocks establishes beyond question, however, is that kids can learn to write about new substance and in new forms by talking together while working through problems designed to provide rehearsals for the kind of thinking they will have to do when they are writing. This insight is corroborated by Andrews and his colleagues (2009), whose synthesis of studies demonstrates the effectiveness of using oral arguments in preparation for written ones. Little wonder. In our teaching careers we've often heard teachers lament that their kids can't write but have never yet heard a complaint that they can't talk. So one reason that we emphasize composing instead of writing is that we want to use students' oral abilities to support their writing.

Another reason we emphasize composing instead of writing is brought home in the research of Peter Smagorinsky (see, for example, 1995, 1997; Smagorinsky, Pettis, and Reed 2004; Smagorinsky, Zoss, and Reed 2006), whose work calls into question why writing is privileged over other kinds of composing. Peter and his colleagues demonstrate the powerful intellectual engagement of young people as they build models, draw, or choreograph a response to literature, and so on.

Peter's work is focused on alternative modes of composing in school, but it jibes with the work of researchers who are examining students' out-of-school literacies (see, for example, the edited collections of Hull and Schultz [2002] and Mahiri [2004] and the comprehensive review of Cushman, Barbier, Mazak, and Petrone [2006]). As Jeff and Michael (2002) found in their examination of the literate lives of young men both in and out of school, young people are deeply involved in literate activity, even those who reject traditional school literacies. In short, we firmly believe that student engagement in out-of-school literacies is far too valuable a resource to ignore.

Composing to Practice

Perhaps the most significant difference between our instructional emphasis here and that which typifies the teaching of writing in schools is our emphasis on composing to practice. In our experience, most composition instruction, at least in classrooms that aren't writing workshops, begins with an assignment. As we noted earlier, the instruction that follows characteristically seeks to develop declarative knowledge of form (through the assignment itself, a rubric, the study of models, or the study of traditional school grammar) or declarative knowledge of substance (through the reading and discussion of a text). In writing workshop classes students undoubtedly get more instruction, either through minilessons or coaching. But here, too, that instruction is done in service of the particular piece of writing the student is doing.

Rather than the traditional instruction that emphasizes declarative knowledge or the responsive kind of teaching that characterizes writing workshops, we'll be calling for anticipatory teaching in order to develop the procedural knowledge to be successful on particular writing tasks in particular writing contexts. We'll stress composing to practice by beginning with a focus not on the particular piece on which students are working but rather with a focus on the particular kind of writing we ask students to do, in this case, argument. As you'll see, our lessons are designed to give students extended practice in miniature so that they can develop the procedural knowledge they will need. That is, we want to give them plenty of opportunities in developing claims that are reasonable and debatable, in finding and generating data that provide a safe starting point, in articulating warrants that effectively connect the data to the claim, and in anticipating and responding to counterarguments. Only then will we move to providing more targeted preparation for particular kinds of argument.

We see composing as similar to most other human activities. If you're going to become expert at it, you need to practice. In an article in *The New York Times Magazine* Dubner and Levitt (2006) reported that studies of expertise, which include investigations of such different activities as "soccer, golf, surgery, piano playing, Scrabble, writing, chess, software design, stock picking and darts" (par. 7) make

> a rather startling assertion: the trait we commonly call talent is highly overrated. Or, put another way, expert performers— whether in memory or surgery, ballet or computer programming—are nearly always made, not born. And yes, practice does make perfect. (par. 8)

As Michael (Smith 2007) has explained elsewhere, providing practice is most effective when it moves in at least one of the following directions:

- From the immediate to the imagined
- From the short to the long

- From the oral to the written

- From the scaffolded to the independent

- From the social to the independent

Rather than talk about each of these directions in the abstract, we'll highlight them in our discussion of lessons throughout the rest of the book. Suffice it to say at this time, though, that we want students to have lots and lots of practice and to experience lots and lots of success before we ask them to take on an assignment.

Composing to Plan

For Collins, composing to plan, what he calls writing to capture ideas, is brainstorming. We think that composing to plan involves much more than that.

In the first place, composing to plan involves articulating as clearly as possible what you hope to accomplish in your writing given the context in which that writing is situated. That articulation needs to happen before any other kind of composing can occur.

But even after students have articulated their purposes, planning is likely to require much more than brainstorming. As we hope we made clear in our discussion of out-of-school literacies, we think it's critically important for teachers to make good use of the resources students bring with them to class. That said, we worry about the extent to which brainstorming has become the dominant mode of prewriting that students are asked to do because it presumes that students already know all that they need to know in order to write.

If only that were true for us. Although we almost always write about educational issues we know something about, we never know enough. We always have additional work to do, sometimes through reading and sometimes through designing ways to collect new data. As we noted in our discussion of the five kinds of knowledge, procedural knowledge of substance, understanding how to get the stuff about which we'll write, that is, understanding how to inquire, is at the very heart of what we do as writers.

Sure, there's a place for brainstorming. But as you'll see, there's also a place for developing heuristics for what Stuart Greene (1992) calls "mining texts in reading to write." There's also a place for composing interview questions or surveys or observational protocols. Composing to plan involves unearthing both the new and the known. If we want to prepare our students for college, we have to help them develop procedural knowledge of substance. We have to teach them how to get the stuff about which they will write.

First Draft Composing

According to American journalist Gene Fowler, "Writing is easy: All you do is sit staring at a blank sheet of paper until drops of blood form on your forehead." Pretty funny until you realize that if you Google "fear of the blank page," you'll get over 3.6 million hits. These hits include a blog posting entitled "Fear of a Blank Page" by Ian Ingram that begins this way:

> How long would you guess I stared at this screen after typing that title? Three days. It took me three days to push one key, to lay down that first "H" back there. The title was in reference to starting a new piece but the concept seems to be contagious and has spread to this blog. This is my first entry since the creation of the blog (I wrote the small essays about my new works before this blog was built) and because it's the first it feels *important*. Hesitation begets hesitation. Right when you need to commit and jump into something this nefarious disease strikes. Stagnation, procrastination and doubt crawl out from their burrows and begin circling.

We know that lots and lots of students are stymied by those first words. So we have to give them lots and lots of practice getting started. We have to help them overcome the hesitation, stagnation, procrastination, and doubt that Ingram chronicles. If we're to do so, we have to provide more than a couple of opportunities each quarter to begin.

Final Draft Composing

Once students have completed their drafts, we want to give them instruction in polishing and publishing their work. What we mean by final draft composing comprises the last three of Collins' five kinds of writing: edit for focus correction areas, edit for focus correction area after peer response, and publish.

As you'll see, once again we work to make sure that students have the procedural knowledge they will need. That's why we provide more than the opportunity to polish and publish. We also provide instruction in how to do so. In our experience students often conflate revising with making sentence-level corrections. Sentence-level corrections are important, but so too are making substantive additions and deletions. So too is restructuring an argument to enhance its effectiveness. So too is evaluating what besides words can increase the power of the presentation. Students need instruction and practice in each of these areas.

Composing to Transfer

As we noted previously, Toulmin (1958) understands that particular contexts provide particular challenges for composers of arguments. Factoring in disciplinary differences, and the almost infinite variations possible in different immediate contexts, reveals that teaching to transfer is crucial. Students need to understand what about arguments stays the same regardless of context and what doesn't and therefore needs to be adapted.

In fact, as we've argued elsewhere (Smith and Wilhelm 2006, 2010), we believe the issue of transfer is perhaps the single most important issue we need to address as teachers. We need always to think about how what we do today prepares students for their next class, their other subjects, their composing outside school, and their educational futures.

Our hard thinking is crucially important because the evidence on transfer paints a pretty bleak picture. Haskell (2000) puts it this way: "Despite the importance of transfer of learning, research findings over the past nine decades clearly show that as individuals, and as educational institutions, we have failed to achieve transfer of learning on any significant level" (xiii).

According to Haskell (2000), if our students are to transfer what they've learned, they have to have deep understanding of what is to be transferred and they have to get plenty of practice in applying meaning-making and problem-solving principles to new situations. Too often, we think, teachers subscribe to what Perkins and Salomon (1988) call the Little Bo Peep view of transfer; that is, if we "leave them alone" our students will come to a new task and automatically transfer relevant knowledge and skills. Instead, they argue that if we want students to apply what they learn in new contexts that differ from the ones in which they initially learned the material, we have to give them conscious control over what they have learned. They call this *high-road transfer*. We think of it this way, "If you can name it, then you can move it."

Let's do a thought experiment: Have you ever had to do work on an unfamiliar word processing program, maybe even a more recent version of a program you're familiar with? Plenty of moves that you make will be automatic. Typing, for example. But Little Bo Peep won't always prevail. If you can't find a function that you're used to on a toolbar, you have to be able to reason about it. You'll find yourself saying such things as, "Okay, here's where it was in the past and here's what other functions it was placed with. So let me look here." That is, you'll have to be mindful about what you know. You'll have to exercise conscious control. Our instruction is designed to help students develop that conscious control about argumentation.

Before we move on, a couple of notes. First, although we believe that any effective writing curriculum will include all five kinds of composing, we want to stress that we don't see them as suggesting a rigid sequence. We're not saying first you practice, then you plan, then you draft, then you polish, then you work on transfer. As you'll see in the chapters that follow, we see it as a more iterative and recursive process.

Second, although we're pleased with the neatness of building our instruction on five kinds of writing and five kinds of composing, we want to stress that our lists do not have a one-to-one correspondence. Composing to practice can be directed at procedural knowledge of form, or procedural knowledge of substance, or both. Composing to practice may be directed to developing procedural understandings that are useful across contexts or it may be directed toward addressing particular aspects of the immediate situation or wider environment. Composing to plan could include practice in finding or generating data that would be useful across contexts or it could include planning for purpose and a specific context. Both first- and final-draft composing require all five kinds of knowledge working in concert. And if students are to transfer what they've learned we have to help them develop an articulated understanding of all five kinds of knowledge.

Our major point in this chapter is that for students to deeply understand how to write or read anything, they need to exercise and develop all five kinds of knowledge, and that they can do so through engaging in all five kinds of composing. We hope that the distinctions we make here help you look hard at your curriculum and your instruction to make sure that you're helping students develop all the knowledge that they need and that you're providing sufficient practice in all of the kinds of composing they'll need to do. We hope that the new CCSS and attendant assessments provide an incentive for taking that hard look at our practice as we work to develop the deep and transferable knowledge about writing and reading our students need. Finally, we hope that this chapter provides a lens through which you examine the rest of this book. It's time we put our money where our mouths are.

Implications for Planning and Practice

Just as we think that the five kinds of knowledge and five kinds of composing provide a useful lens for you to use in evaluating the instructional ideas we'll be proposing in the rest of the book, so too do we think that they can be useful lenses for you to use in examining your own practice. The inservice and preservice teachers with whom we have worked have found them to be so.

So before moving on to the next chapter, think about the last writing assignment you gave and ask yourself whether you engaged your students in instruction that helped them understand not only what they were writing about and the form that you wanted that writing to take, but also how to generate content and how to produce the formal features of the writing. Ask yourself if you created a context that required students to appeal to a real audience for a real purpose. Ask yourself if you gave them plenty of practice, enough so that you were pretty sure they would be successful. Ask yourself if you helped them understand how to get started and what they could accomplish through revision. Ask if you provided the opportunity for them to reflect on the work they did and then apply what they learned to new tasks, both academic and real-world ones.

We realize that we're setting the bar pretty high here and we didn't always jump over it ourselves when we were teaching, as one story of bad teaching we have done will illustrate.

When Michael was teaching, his school required that all juniors had to write a research paper. Michael decided that he wanted to make a connection between writing the research paper and the rest of his American Literature class, so he assigned students to write about an American artist of the twentieth century.

Michael began his instruction as he had been taught, by providing a schedule for when the various components of the paper were due, by showing students the school's bibliographic form, and by providing a model for writing an information card. He worked with individuals when the class went to the library (no Internet connections then) to help them find information and refine their topics.

When he collected the information cards, he was baffled. Just what did they have in mind when they wrote out these cards, he wondered. When he read the final drafts, he found his answer: Nothing really. The papers were, by and large, more like bad encyclopedia entries than anything he wanted to read. And not only that, they didn't even follow the correct form.

Tempting as it is to blame his students, Michael now understands that their failures were his fault. He really only focused on one kind of knowledge—declarative knowledge of form—and assumed (wrongly) that students would gain declarative knowledge of substance through their reading. He focused a little on composing to plan when he looked at their information cards and more on final draft composing in the many hours he spent responding to their papers.

Over the following years he worked to do a better job. He divided his students into small groups to read a text together and determine what information was most worth citing and then how they'd cite it (procedural knowledge of form and substance). He asked them to write about topics that mattered (for example, school policies) and asked readers who mattered to respond to them (knowledge of context).

Before students investigated their own topic, they all wrote a short research paper on whether Holden Caulfield, the main character in the novel *The Catcher in the Rye*, which the class had just finished reading, was a typical adolescent using research Michael had done (procedural knowledge of form; composing to practice). They discussed criteria for evaluation and then applied those criteria to their own and their classmates' work (first draft and final draft composing). They applied what they learned to writing a public policy argument (composing to transfer). Were those papers perfect? Nope. Were they better? Absolutely. In short, the importance of the five kinds of knowledge and five kinds of composing have been borne out in our teaching. We hope you find them equally useful.

CHAPTER 4

Making Argument Matter in the Here and Now

One of the key findings of *"Reading Don't Fix No Chevys"* (Smith and Wilhelm 2002), Michael and Jeff's study of the literate lives of young men both in and out of school, is that the young men in the study valued the activities they most liked for the immediate enjoyment they took from them rather than for what benefits those activities might bring them in the future. The boys played sports because they enjoyed them, not to win a scholarship, to impress others, or to get more fit. They watched TV or movies because TV and movies made them laugh or kept them on the edge of their seats. They wrote or drew or rapped or designed websites because of the joy they took in the creative process and their enjoyment in sharing what they had created with others. They listened to music, the most popular activity across the young men, because doing so helped them focus on the moment. Here's Stan:

> Lately I've been listening to a couple hardcore bands, Vision
> of Disorder, and um Machine Head and stuff like that. I like
> listening to Vision of Disorder when I'm really mad because it
> helps me just like feel what I'm actually feeling.

As Maurice explained, the root of his enjoyment of video games was very similar:

> Say you're having a problem with someone or whatever. You
> play a video game or it's like a shooting game or airplane flying
> game. You have to take the mission. That helps you take your
> mind off the stuff that's going on in your life, and you just, for
> that ten or twenty—-for however long you play the game—, it

helps you forget that. It helps you relieve your mind from that
and focus yourself on the game.

This inclination to focus on the immediate, one that was displayed by the boys in Michael and Jeff's study and one that we have all seen in many of the young women we have taught as well, creates a profound irony for us as teachers. It is our obligation to prepare our students for the future. But we are convinced that we can only do so if we can engage them in the present. In the case of teaching students to read and write arguments, that should be easy. But we're afraid it's not.

Why should it be easy? As we noted in Chapter 1, the CCSS justify their emphasis on argumentation by noting that arguments are at the heart of academic disciplines. And as Michael and Jeff (Smith and Wilhelm 2006) found, young people want to develop "the competence and capacities of real experts." That is, they want to be able to knowingly engage in those critical disciplinary arguments. The young men Michael and Jeff studied

> wanted to solve problems, debate, and argue in ways through
> which they could stake their identity and develop both ideas
> and functional tools that they could share and use with others
> in very immediate ways. (57)

Moreover, as we also explained in Chapter 1, arguments are endemic in our culture. If we make links between students' lives and what we want them to learn, we would almost have to draw on some of the myriad ongoing cultural conversations that are argumentative at their core.

But although arguments are endemic in the academy and in the culture, they are strangely absent in English language arts classrooms. Indeed, Applebee, Langer, Nystrand, and Gamoran's (2003) analysis of twenty seventh- to twelfth-grade classrooms found that what they call *open-discussion*, defined as "more than 30 seconds of free exchange of ideas among students or between at least three participants" which "usually begins in response to an open-ended question about which students can legitimately disagree" (707) averaged 1.7 minutes per 60 minutes of class time. So according to Applebee and his colleagues, students rarely have an opportunity to assert and defend their positions on an issue that's debatable, which, as we explained in Chapter 2, is one of the essential conditions for claims in arguments. A pretty depressing finding and one that's clearly at odds with our students' best interests and the likelihood that they'll be able to meet the demands of the CCSS, for as Applebee and his colleagues found at both the middle and high school levels "high academic demands and discussion-based approaches were significantly related to literacy performance" (722).

Why do discussions remain closed in light of such findings? We think that the persistence of teacher-dominated, close-ended classroom discourse is rooted in an observation Andrews and his colleagues (2009) make about British education that we think applies equally to the United States: "Most English teachers, at primary or secondary level, still see a literary core to their practice, values and professional training" (292). Teachers teach texts that they love or at least that they think are important. It makes sense, then, to try to help students see just what it is about those texts that makes us and/or the culture value them. Moreover, as Peter Rabinowitz (Rabinowitz and Smith 1998) explains, we typically teach texts that we have read many times to kids who are reading them for the first time. We've settled at least many of the potential open-ended questions we could ask.

As a consequence, it's hard to break the pattern of discourse that typifies discussions of literature, as Marshall (Marshall, Smagorinsky, and Smith 1995) found, even for teachers who strive to do so. It seems to us, therefore, that we need to do something to necessitate breaking the mold, both on our part and on our students'. The most powerful way we have found for doing this is to embed our instruction in inquiry units that focus on essential questions.

Essential questions are the big and enduring questions that are likely to have brought us to the profession in the first place, questions like "What makes me, me?," "Can people understand each other across demographic differences?," "What does it mean to be heroic?" We could go on with other examples but we won't as we've written about this idea at length elsewhere (Smith and Wilhelm 2006; Wilhelm 2007; Wilhelm and Novak 2011).

But we do want to share a personal testimonial. Through his whole career, Jeff has kept a teaching journal that chronicles what building units around essential questions has meant for him. Here's one entry:

> Somehow I've lost sight of teaching purposefully. I've just been assigning stuff and letting the curriculum or anthology be my guide. Asking the essential question moves me from teaching a bunch of texts to using a variety of materials to consider and really explore an exciting and important issue!

We've developed essential questions in four primary ways. The first is to take note of the questions that seem to foster energetic exchange in our lives and in our culture. We've spent countless hours over our lives talking about what sustains and interferes with relationships, what makes a good parent or partner or friend, to what we owe our primary allegiance. Political discourse in our country regularly focuses on the question of what our obligation to others is, whether and when the ends justify the means, and so on. If a question can sustain conversation in our lives, it can certainly also do so in our classrooms.

A second approach is to think hard about what makes a required text worth teaching. For example, when Jeff was teaching seventh graders he was required to teach *The Incredible Journey*. When he thought about the issue that was at the heart of the book, he developed the question, "What makes something (an animal, person, species, or culture) survive?"

Another approach is to reframe a standard or cumulative progress indicator. For example, one of the ninth-grade standards delineated by the CCSS for the reading of literature is "Analyze how complex characters (e.g., those with multiple or conflicting motivations) develop over the course of a text, interact with other characters." Among the many possible essential questions motivated by this standard is "Why is it that some people can turn their lives around and others can't?"

➤ *CCSS connection*

Finally, we try to study our own reading to articulate the issues that attract our attention. In fact, the genesis of the question we want to share with you was informed by a news item Michael read in 2004. Here's a synopsis from cnn.com:

> The Arabic-language TV network Al-Jazeera broadcast videotape Saturday showing two French journalists who apparently have been taken hostage in Iraq by a group calling itself the Islamic Army in Iraq. The journalists, Christian Chesnot with Radio France International and Georges Malbrunot with the newspaper *Le Figaro*, were reported missing the morning of August 21. It was not known where they were being held. According to Al-Jazeera, the kidnappers are demanding that the French government overturn a recently passed law that bans Muslim students from wearing head-scarves in French public schools.

Michael's immediate response upon reading the item was something like this: "The stupid French government!" But then, "Wait, it's the Islamic Army that's at fault." And then, "No, it's the U.S. invasion of Iraq." Or maybe: "It's the newspapers or even the journalists themselves." At every turn Michael assigned responsibility for the kidnapping to a different person or institution. His experience of reading the news story led him to this question: "To what extent are people responsible for what happens to them?"

If we recognize that authentic questions are rare in English language arts classrooms, we also have to realize that we may have to convince students that we don't have preformulated answers in mind. One way to do so is to demonstrate to students that adults take radically different perspectives on the question. A unit in *Hampton-Brown Edge*, an anthology series on which Michael worked (Moore, Short, Smith, and Tatum 2007) that's built around a similar question begins with this quote from Albert Einstein, "Everything is determined, the beginning as well as the end, by forces over which we have no control," and this one by Oprah Winfrey: "With every experience, you alone are painting your own canvas, thought by thought, choice by choice." Students have to see that you can't have it both ways, that no one answer is going to easily carry the day.

To further that understanding, Michael developed the two little stories in Figure 4.1.

We've used the stories in many different contexts and the results are always the same. Some will assign responsibility to the perpetrators, Chris and Joan. Some will assign it to the victims. Some will assign it to the adults in the scene and others to the kids. Some will posit other institutions, for example, the schools or individuals, for example, Joan's parents or caregivers. Some will see the stories as essentially similar and others will see them as different and will therefore assign different proportions of responsibility to parallel characters (the new kid and Maria, Chris and Joan, Devin and the kids on the bus, the coach and the bus driver). And in the ensuing discussion, they will have to explain their positions in fully formed arguments by citing textual evidence (e.g., the new kid drank the liquor) and a warrant (e.g., ultimately people are responsible for what happens to them) and by anticipating and responding to counterarguments (I know that coaches are supposed to be able to control their teams, but you can't be with your team at all times).

When we teach these stories and a difference of opinion emerges, we make sure that students talk to one another and not to us. We orchestrate the conversation by saying things like "Tell him/her why he/she is wrong" to establish that we expect and welcome respectful arguments and by using the phrases that cue the development of data ("What makes you say so?") and warrants ("So what? Why is that important to your argument?").

Figure 4.1

In each of the little stories that follow, something bad happens to one of the characters. As you read the story, think about who's responsible and when you've finished assign each character the percent of the responsibility he or she is responsible for. If you think someone or something else is responsible, add that person or thing to your assignment of responsibility. Your percentages should end up equaling 100 percent. Be sure that you are able to justify why and how you assigned responsibility in the way that you did.

1. If you wanted to play varsity basketball, you knew what was in store for you during summer practice: the initiation. At the end of preseason practice, each new team member was taken out by three or four more experienced teammates to be "toughened up." Sometimes that took the form of being left alone in the woods in nothing but underwear. Sometimes it took the form of being made to eat the grisly kind of stuff people have to eat on Survivor. Sometimes it took the form of more physical things, like being hit with a paddle. And it seems that the better the young player, the worse the initiation. It might be tough, but the kids on the team say that it helps the team bond. And it's hard to argue with success: the team has made the state tournament each of the last 5 years. This year, however, the administration said that it was cracking down on hazing. The said they had a zero tolerance policy and that anyone who was caught hazing would be expelled. Even before the new policy, Devin, one of the team's best players and the only senior on the team had decided that this year he wouldn't participate, though he didn't tell anyone. But the other lettermen thought it was up to them to continue the tradition. Devin did go last year, though. He didn't make the new players do anything, but he had to admit that he thought it was funny when the others made the new players run up to the coach's door wearing only their jockstraps and ring the doorbell. Devin was glad he wasn't going this year. He was a bit worried about one of the kids who was initiated last year, a kid named Chris. Chris was something of a bully and he had been talking all year about what it was going to be like for the new kids once he had a chance to do the initiating. Chris said he wasn't letting any policy stop him. On the night of the initiation Devin got a call from the coach. The coach told Devin that he was going to kick one of new players off the team because the kid had been found by police passed out in a drunken stupor. The coach said the kid was so drunk that he had to be taken to the hospital, but that the kid would make it. When Devin saw Chris the next day, Chris just smirked and said, "I guess some people just can't hold their liquor." Devin wondered about the other kids who were initiated. And he wondered if it was just coincidence that the kid who had been found drunk played the same position that Chris did.

Who's responsible for what happened to the new kid?

_____ Devin　　_____ Chris　　_____ The new kid　　_____ The coach

_____ other (Please specify_____)

2. Day after day Maria had to put up with the same stuff from Joan. Jokes about her accent. Jokes about her clothes. It was the worst on the bus in the morning when Joan would give a loud monologue about her. Most of the kids on the bus seemed scared of Joan, who was a real bully. They laughed nervously, even the couple of kids with whom Maria had gotten friendly in the two weeks she had been in the school. Maria's face burned, but she never said anything. She didn't want to get in a fight, especially since fighting meant suspension. But one day she just couldn't take it anymore. She had an armful of books, and as she was walking down the bus' steps, Joan gave her a shove. All the kids saw it. Books and papers flew everywhere. Maria scrambled to pick them up. As she was picking up her history book, Joan pushed her again and shouted, "Spic! When you're done cleaning here you can come over and clean my bathroom." Maria didn't want to fight, but these actions and this language were more than she could take. She ran up to Joan, pushed her as hard as she could, and punched her in the face when she was on the ground. She would have hit her again, but she was dragged away by a teacher. Now she's suspended for a week, the minimum required by the school's antiviolence policy. And Joan is still going to school! Maria just can't believe it. She's not sure she'll ever go back.

Who's responsible for Maria's suspension?

_____ Maria　　_____ Joan　　_____ The bus driver　　_____ The other kids on the bus

_____ other (Please specify_____)

➤ *Speaking and listening anchor standards 3, 4, 5; reading anchor standards 1, 2, 8, 9, 10*

Where you'd go next would depend on the kids you're teaching, but the key would be to read literary, popular, cultural, and disciplinary texts that take different positions on the question. For example, in *Romeo and Juliet* Shakespeare would seem to say people aren't responsible for what happens to them: "From forth the fatal loins of these two foes / A pair of star-cross'd lovers. . . ." Although *West Side Story* tells a very similar story, Stephen Sondheim seems to take a different position. In the satiric "Gee, Officer Krupke," the Jets, and Sondheim, are poking fun at those who would attribute the gang's actions to a "social disease." According to Sondheim, it seems, the responsibility for the gangs' actions resides with them. Think of the other texts you could use to have your kids think hard about who's responsible for the child sexual abuse scandal at Penn State, the Holocaust, the subprime mortgage crisis, the devastation of Hurricane Katrina, the steroid era in baseball, and on and on.

In our appendix we present a unit developed by Brandon Bolyard and Cecilia Patte, two Fellows of the Boise State Writing Project so you can see how an entire unit built around an essential question that also features extended attention to argumentation might be organized. Just how you'll design your unit will of course depend on your teaching context, but a unit on the question "To what extent are people responsible for what happens to them?" could begin something like this:

➤ *Lesson ideas*

- Day 1: Have Einstein and Winfrey quotes displayed in some fashion and ask students to write in their journal with whom they most agree with and why. Discuss scenes.

- Day 2: Have students do responsibility ratings for one or two relevant current events. Homework: Have students bring in a newspaper, magazine, or Internet report on another current event they'd like to discuss.

- Day 3: Small group work on student selected texts. Whole-class discussion to begin developing an anchor chart on criteria used to determine responsibility.

- Day 4: Read short literary text that takes up the issue. Have students do responsibility ranking from their perspective, the perspective of different characters, and the author.

- Day 5: Writing workshop. Have students choose one of the issues/ texts the class has discussed and develop an argument justifying their ranking. (Note: this activity presumes that at least some of the preparatory work that we'll describe in Chapters 5–7 has already been done.)

Let's consider the benefits of engaging students in extended consideration of essential questions in inquiry units that involve the reading of both literature and other kinds of texts. A recent conceptual review of research on teaching the reading and writing of argument by George Newell and his colleagues (Newell, Beach, Smith, VanDerHeide, 2011) makes two crucial points that would seem to endorse such an approach. They argue that

> One limitation of the traditional one-shot persuasive essay assignment is that there is little ongoing development of arguments and counterarguments surrounding writing such essays; students have no reason to explore counterarguments, because they often do not receive counterarguments from the teacher and, therefore, have no reason for doing so. (292)

This critique is especially damning, as Newell and his colleagues point out, because research establishes that a writer's consideration of counterarguments results in higher quality essays and "more favorable perceptions of the writer" (282). Inquiry units have argument and counterargument at their very core.

Because inquiry units built around essential questions involve extended reading, writing, and talking about texts that address a similar issue, students have an opportunity to develop both the declarative and procedural knowledge that they need. All of the reading, writing, and talking that students do acts as a kind of frontloading (Wilhelm, Baker, and Dube-Hackett 2001) for the reading, writing, and talking they will do in the future. For example, a discussion of the first scene above would provide a rehearsal for the reading of and discussion about a text that took up the responsibility of ordinary Germans for the Holocaust. Likewise, as students go through various readings in a unit, they can return to the frontloading scenes (or any other frontloading activity you try) and can be asked how the author or character would respond to them. In this way, the frontloading becomes a touchstone and template for promoting and place holding their evolving understanding—they are composing to plan and practice.

Moreover, because inquiry units built around essential questions address issues that are important in kids' lives, they can draw on their experience outside school as a source of implication. In talking about the above examples, students will surely talk about their experience on teams or with hazing or with bullies or with buses.

The frontloading and clear links to kids' lives will allow all students to read texts of increasing complexity, a critical component of the CCSS, because they will have the background knowledge they need. As a consequence, they'll have more mental resources to cope with more sophisticated syntax. Inquiry units are also likely to feature repeated exposure to unit-related vocabulary. In a unit that asks the question "To what extent are people responsible for what happens to them?" secondary students encounter words like *responsibility, liability, accountability, fate, destiny, agency,* and so on, which means that they will comprehend those words when they encounter them. These benefits are especially important for our ELL students.

➤ *Reading anchor standard 10, language anchor standards 4–6*

Finally, inquiry units built around essential questions provide the opportunity to use texts of differing difficulties in meaningful ways so that we can meet the needs of our struggling and ELL readers and writers. One of the difficulties with differentiating instruction is creating a common classroom project that honors the contributions of all students. Inquiry units built around essential questions reduce those difficulties. For example, the question "To what extent are people responsible for what happens to them?" seems to us to be one that's explicitly asked by *The Cat in the Hat.* And if one uses a children's book in service of considering a very important and very adult question, then the students who are struggling with the language, and who might be embarrassed to read in class what they are able to read, are doing manifestly adult work.

Reading different kinds of texts is also important for our students. The review by Newell and his colleagues (2011) note that Crowhurst's (1990) research strongly suggests the value of integrating the reading and writing of arguments. This finding jibes with the increasing attention in the profession to mentor texts (see, for example, Robb 2010), those texts that students study as a way to learn some aspect(s) of the writer's craft. To be sure, literary narratives of various sorts can serve as mentor texts (take a look at the work done by the Northern Nevada Writing Project at http://writingfix.com/picture_book_prompts.htm), but students who will be writing arguments and who will be considering the extent to which arguments vary by context will surely benefit from reading, studying, and applying what they have learned from reading lots of different arguments.

Because this and the rest of our chapters are centered on our instructional and curricular ideas, we won't close with a separate "Implications for Planning and Practice" subhead as we did in our first three chapters. Instead, we'll close with an exhortation: We have to recognize that if we want to prepare students for their future education, for the workplace, and for their lives—if we want them to meet or even exceed the CCSS—we have to help them become better at reading and composing arguments. To do so will require much more than the occasional persuasive writing assignment. It will require our making argument central to the work we do. Inquiry units built around essential questions do just that.

Introducing the Elements of Argument

We closed our last chapter by claiming that if we want to help our students meet or exceed the CCSS, and in so doing help prepare them for their future education, for the workplace, and for their lives, we have to make argument central to the work we do. But as we argued in Chapter 3, we have to do much more than provide the opportunity for argument. We have to provide instruction to help students develop the procedural (of form and substance), declarative (of form and substance), and contextual knowledge that they need.

Introducing Toulmin's Model

➤ *Lesson idea* ### Through Talk

We suggest starting with procedural and declarative knowledge of form, by which we mean working to help students understand and be able to produce the elements of argument that we introduced in Chapter 2. And we think the place to start is through talk. By talking, students can tap into the existing knowledge they possess to develop new knowledge while at the same time seeing that what they're learning has a payoff in their lives.

We began our units by talking with students about music, movies, sports, and school rules; all things our students cared about. When we did, we consistently used the same language to cue the various elements of Toulmin's model. A conversation about who's the best rapper ever might go something like this (we used the entries at www.the-top-tens.com/lists/best-rapper-of-all-time.asp to generate possible student responses):

T: Who's the best rapper of all time?

S1: Eminem's the best.

T: What makes you say so?

S1: His lyrics are the best.

T: What makes you say so?

S1: He has a song for whatever mood you're in. "Till I Collapse" pumps me up and "Just Lose It" makes me laugh.

T: So what?

S1: What do you mean, "So what?"

T: I mean why does it matter that Eminem has different kinds of songs?

S1: Well only the best rappers can have great songs of different kinds.

T: What about the folks who say that his lyrics are bad because they degrade women?

S1: That's mostly Slim Shady. He's a character, not Eminem.

T: Everyone agree?

S2: No, that's crazy. It's Tupac.

T: What makes you say so?

S2: He's the most influential rapper of all time.

T: What makes you say so?

S2: He just is.

T: Well, he's not the best selling.

S2: Yeah, but his raps are about stuff that matters, like "Keep Ya Head Up" starts by talking about respecting women. Unlike Eminem.

T: So what?

S2: It doesn't get any better than rapping for the people.

T: But what about the people who say he hurt rap instead of helped it because of that East Coast–West Coast thing he was into.

S2: Yeah maybe but many more of his songs were about making change and making things better. That's why his music is taught in college classes.

We could go on, but we hope you get the idea. In fact, when we taught, we'd go on for at least an entire period, sometimes more. What inevitably began to happen is that students would anticipate the questions and form responses to them before they were asked. They'd work to avoid being asked, "What makes you say so?" by providing more detailed and less problematic data. They would try to avoid the dreaded "So what?" by making clear connections between their data and their claims. They began to anticipate possible rebuttals to their claim and to respond to those rebuttals even before they were offered.

After we argued, we'd go back to the arguments that we had had to introduce and define Toulmin's terms (though we might substitute *evidence* or *support* for *data* or *connection* for *warrant*, depending on our students) and illustrate them by reference to the arguments we had had as a class. Figure 5.1 displays how we could use the chart we introduced in Chapter 2 to provide that illustration.

In Chapter 3 we talked about the relationship between procedural and declarative knowledge, drawing on Vygotsky to argue that declarative knowledge can only be developed through procedural engagement. That's why we always suggest

➤ *Speaking and listening anchor standards 1, 4, and 6*

➤ *Speaking and listening anchor standard 3*

Figure 5.1

Data:

Answers the question, "What makes you say so?" Has to provide a safe starting point.

Tupac's raps are about stuff that matters, like "Keep Ya Head Up" starts by talking about respecting women.

Connection:

Answers the question, "So what?"

It doesn't get any better than rapping for the people.

Claim:

The starting point for an argument. Must be clear, defensible, and controversial.

Tupac's the best rapper ever.

Unless

Response:

Explains why the counterargument does not overcome the claim.

Many more of his songs were about making change and making things better. That's why his music is taught in college classes.

Counterargument:

What someone who disagrees might say.

But he contributed to the East Coast–West Coast conflict that left people dead.

that you introduce terms through labeling what a student has already done rather than beginning with a term and a definition. And we want to stress that it's crucial to keep in mind that using Toulmin's model is a means to the end of helping students become more proficient composers and consumers of arguments. That is, while we introduced the terms and used them, we never tested students on them. What mattered to us was that students understood how to employ them rather than how to define them.

Two more notes on terms before we move on. First, as Karen Lundsford (2002) points out, we have to be cognizant of the instructional context in which we're operating. Students, at least secondary students, bring a vocabulary about writing to our classes. So it's worth the time to talk about how Toulmin's terms might relate to ones they already know. *Claim* maps on pretty well to *thesis*, at least in most cases. *Data* and *warrant* (or *connection*) are kinds of support. The most significant difference between Toulmin's terms and what students are likely to have encountered in other classes is the term *reason*. In Michael's school, for example, some colleagues used the heuristic FIRE (fact-incident-reason-example) as a way to teach students how to support their ideas. But the reasons students provided (e.g., Tupac's the best because he's the most influential) typically did not provide the kind of safe starting points that they needed to. Rather, they were what might be called *data-claims*. That is, they were subclaims that students needed to establish before they provided the safe starting point that would allow them to move forward.

Second, we're aware that at this point we haven't advocated introducing the notion that, at least to some extent, arguments are context-dependent. We could have, for example, by asking students whether their arguments would change depending on their relationship with their interlocutors or their interlocutor's knowledge of rap, or age, or gender, or race. We made the judgment that it makes sense to begin with the field-invariant elements before adding this complication, though as you'll see, we think discussion of context should come soon.

Through Ads

> *Lesson idea*

Our students are exposed to ads everywhere they go, both in actual and in virtual spaces. We've found that engaging students in analyzing, critiquing, and producing ads is an excellent way for them to develop and demonstrate their understanding of arguments. We suggest beginning by sharing a print or video ad of a product that kids are likely to care about. It's important to choose one that draws on some kind of data as one way to achieve its impact. For example, you could begin a class by showing a video about a new style of basketball shoes. We found one on YouTube that features Derrick Rose, the Chicago Bulls player who won the 2010–2011 Most Valuable Player Award in the NBA, advertising Adidas. The ad intersperses Rose's making spectacular plays on the basketball court with images of his walking Chicago's streets. The voice-over is Rose, who begins by saying, "Remember this number: 9.8." He continues by saying that it's not the seconds on the shot clock, or how much time is remaining in the game, or the number of times "I will light you up." No, he says, 9.8 refers to the ounces that "makes this the lightest [shoe] ever."

The next step would be to analyze the ad by asking, "What is Derrick Rose trying to convince us of? What's his claim?" Students will respond quickly: "To buy the adiZero basketball shoe." Then you can probe using the kinds of questions you used in the initial conversation: "What makes him say so?" Answer: "At 9.8 ounces they're the lightest basketball shoes." So what? The warrant of the ad's argument goes unstated, so it's tricky, but after some time students are likely to say something like "Light shoes are good shoes." You could probe and ask why and they'd likely quickly respond that lighter shoes will reduce fatigue or allow players to jump higher.

Thus far the class discussion isn't an authentic one in that there are a limited number of appropriate answers to the questions. But now the discussion can become more authentic. You can ask, "Is that true?" Is weight what really matters? Some students might agree and others wouldn't. We'd suggest tracking the range of competing warrants students might provide. Cost, support, and durability are likely to be suggested.

Then you can ask, "Who do you think the audience of this ad is?" It seems to us that the answer is young men and you'll likely receive that answer, but whether you receive that answer or a different one or a more specific one (e.g., urban adolescents who are serious players), we suggest following up with the same probing questions you've been asking: "What makes you say so?" and "So what?" Then we suggest turning to the alternative warrants that students posed and ask them to suggest an audience or audiences for whom that warrant would be appealing.

It seems to us that the ad is making a concurrent argument, as do all ads that have celebrity spokespeople. Putting it in Toulmin's terms, the piece of data is

"Derrick Rose uses these shoes." The implied warrant is something like "If you wear the same shoes, you'll be as good as he is." Or maybe, "He's so good, he'd only wear the best." We don't want to spend too much time talking about an ad you may not use. But you could go through essentially the same procedures regardless of the ad you choose.

➤ *CCSS speaking and listening anchor standard 2*

The next step is to divide students into groups of two or three and to give each group a magazine and the following assignment:

➤ *Lesson idea*

Find three (or two or four depending on your students) ads and answer the following questions:

1. What's the ad trying to convince people of? What's the claim?

2. What evidence does the ad provide? How does the ad answer the "What makes you say so?" question?

3. What's the answer to the "So what?" question? (Remember the answer to "So what?" is often unstated.)

4. Who's the audience for the ad? Make sure you use your answer to the "What makes you say so?" and "So what?" questions when you explain.

5. How would the ad have been different if it had had a different audience?

6. Which of your ads is most effective? What makes you say so?

➤ *Speaking and listening anchor standard 1, 2, and 3*

As a quick illustration, the back cover of the *Newsweek* Michael received as he was drafting this chapter features a full-page ad for Newton Fruit Thins, a new cookie. The visual is a cookie with a bite out of it sitting atop blueberries and raw grains. The text reads, "Introducing Blueberry Brown Sugar Newton Fruit Thins. Real blueberries. 8 grams of whole grains. It's ONE UNIQUE COOKIE." Students who receive this ad might answer the five questions with something like this:

1. Buy the cookie.

2. It has real blueberries and whole grains.

3. You should buy cookies that are good for you.

4. The ad's for parents. They're the ones who care about health. Kids don't.

5. If the ad were for kids it'd maybe show a kid biting into one with a big smile or something like that. Kids care about taste.

Then groups could present the ad they thought was most effective and the one they thought was least effective and explain why. This sharing would be especially effective if your students could display the ad in some way.

One of the really interesting things that inevitably happened in the work we did with ads was that students would get angry because of the results of their analyses. For example, one student was outraged at a car ad that drew on the data that J. D. Power rated the car highest in its class in initial quality. In small print the ad noted that initial quality was judged by the number of complaints in the first twelve months of service. The student's rant went something like this: "Who cares about initial quality? That's a stupid 'so what?' What matters isn't how a car is at the beginning. What matters is how long it lasts!" When students talked about how the ads would change based on the audience, students were once again incensed, exclaiming, "Why is it that ads for adults, at least sometimes, try to be logical? The ones to us never are. They must think we're stupid!"

➤ *Lesson idea*

Finally, we asked students to make their own ads. They could make up a product or create an ad for an existing product. When Michael did this assignment years ago, all of his students made print ads. But now we'd allow them to use any kind of media they chose. Students presented the ads along with a Toulmin diagram analyzing them. Then the class talked about them, focusing on the argument that they made and whether that argument was a logical one or whether the ad was designed to work not on reason but on something else.

➤ *Writing anchor standards 6 and 10*

Before we go on, we want to highlight some of the instructional principles that informed our introductory work. First, our instruction begins by trying to demonstrate to students that what they're learning will matter in the here and now, that it's not just an empty academic exercise, by showing them that what they are learning has clear implications for what they do outside of school. In doing so, we are also giving students a sense of competence. Their ability to compose orally, and in a variety of media, is the springboard to the written argumentation they'll ultimately be doing. Second, we're working on procedural, declarative, and contextual knowledge in concert as that's how we employ them in the real world. Third, we're also putting the consumption of arguments (that is, the reading, viewing, and analysis students did) and the production of arguments (the oral work and the creation of ads) in service of each other. We try not to tip the scales too heavily to one side or the other. Finally, we're giving students lots of practice. Think of how many arguments they would have created or talked about in the matter of a week or so—at least fifty. A far cry from what is characteristic in schools.

Focusing on the Elements of the Model

The work we've described so far helps students be able to employ Toulmin's model. But we've found that a more specific focus on each element of the model is also useful for students. It takes some time, but we think the time is well worth spending, especially if the whole school is relating their work on arguments to Toulmin, something we'd strongly suggest. That way you'd only have to do the introductory work one year and you could begin the others with a much shorter review.

Claims

We suggest beginning with claims. As you may recall from Chapter 2, the critical features of claims is that they are both debatable and defensible. Our students did pretty well developing defensible claims, but when we look back at our teaching we have to admit that we didn't work hard enough to help our students make claims that were debatable, especially when they wrote interpretive arguments about single pieces of literature. Michael looks back and shudders at the number of times he assigned students to write about an issue that was largely settled in class discussion or provided a seemingly open-ended prompt that allowed students to write papers arguing in favor of the obvious, for example, "Choose a character and explain what you think his or her most important personality characteristics are." Reading paper after paper arguing that Atticus in *To Kill a Mockingbird* is courageous or that Holden in *The Catcher in the Rye* hates phonies was his penance for not doing more to help students understand what's worth writing about.

As we argued last chapter and will explore more fully in Chapter 7, embedding writing about literature in inquiry units creates a context for more authentic arguments, but for now we hope we've established that students are taught by school to take safe and easy positions. If we want students to write compelling arguments, we'll have to unteach that survival strategy.

➤ *Lesson idea*

One way to do so is to work with students to develop strategies for testing their claims against the defensible/debatable criteria. We employed Edward de Bono's (1986) work to help us in this effort. De Bono's CoRT program provides sixty lessons designed to help students develop heuristics that they can employ in a variety of contexts. We used the ones in a collection called *Breadth*. We devoted most of our class time to the first tool he introduces, one he calls a PMI (Plus/Minus/Interesting). The PMI lesson calls for students to practice listing all of the possible pluses of a proposed policy, all of the potential minuses, and any consequences that may occur that are not easily placed in either of those two camps. De Bono suggests beginning with policies that are fanciful so that students won't have already formed an opinion (e.g., that people should be required to wear a visible display of the mood they're in). We simply asked students to work individually or together to list as quickly as they could as many pluses, then minuses, then interesting results as they could. We gave them two-minute time limits for each category. So a plus could be, "You wouldn't get your head bit off because you approached someone you didn't know was in a bad mood." A minus: "People might be less apt to try and get out of bad moods if they had to change displays." A potential consequence that's hard to characterize: "More people might start to wear necklaces because that would be one way to show a mood."

After we did a couple of silly ones, we turned to more serious ones and did PMIs on school policies (e.g., requiring every high school graduate to perform a year of community service before starting college or joining the workforce). You could also modify the PMI somewhat for interpretive or evaluative arguments, for example, by asking kids to list all of the support they could provide to argue that their favorite show was the best one on TV and then all of the possible counterarguments that others could make. After this preparation, we could ask students to do a PMI on all of their claims. If a claim didn't have a number of pluses, then it wasn't defensible. If it didn't have at least some minuses, then it wasn't debatable.

In working with students on the PMIs we were not only helping them develop defensible and debatable claims, we were also helping them anticipate and respond to their audience's potential objections, an element of the model we're going to be talking more about later. In fact, one could increase students' attention to the immediate context by having them practice delineating pluses and minuses from particular perspectives. For example, one group of students could develop PMIs for the proposal to require high school graduates to perform a year of service from the perspective of a college, or of the owner of a fast-food store, or the parent of a graduate, or a graduate from an impoverished neighborhood, and so on.

➤ *Writing anchor standard 1; speaking and listening anchor standards 1 and 3*

Data

Once you've spent some time on claims (other de Bono style lessons could usefully be spread across a unit or semester), we suggest moving on to activities that help students develop data. The lessons on data should, we believe, have three foci:

1. Developing a sense of what it means to provide a safe starting point.
2. Identifying the kind of data that would be most useful in making different kinds of claims for different audiences.
3. Generating data.

Determining what's safe. The easy way to encourage students to begin the defense of their claims with data that provides a safe starting point would be to tell them that their data have to be facts or statistics. But that's just not true. For many claims, narratives may be more compelling. Often arguments proceed from the opinion of an authority.

You can engage students in thinking about what data provide a safe starting point by having them evaluate the safety of a variety of data. One way to do so is to employ semantic differential scales. Semantic differential scales are pairs of words that are opposites. A six-point semantic differential scale you could use to have students think about data would look like this:

➤ *Lesson idea*

completely unsafe   completely safe

Students simply mark the scale where they think the data should be placed, as in Figure 5.2.

Once students have filled out a single scale, you can display their assessments easily by drawing a scale on the board or by taping a scale onto the floor of your classroom and having students vote with their feet by standing where they placed each piece of evidence. But what's important is not where they placed each item but rather the discussion and debate about their decisions. That's why

Figure 5.2

Is It Safe?

Each item in the worksheet describes an argument. Rate how likely it is that your audience would regard each piece of data as a safe starting point. Remember, one piece of data is never enough to be persuasive. You're just thinking about whether the piece of data is safe, that is, whether or not the audience would allow you to move on from the data or whether they'd challenge the data and require you to establish it.

1. Claim: *Harry Potter and the Deathly Hallows—Part 2* is the best movie of the year.

    Audience: Classmates

    A. *Harry Potter and the Deathly Hallows—Part 2* made much more money on its first weekend than any other movie ever has.

    completely unsafe   completely safe

    B. When I saw the movie, most of the people didn't leave their seats until after the credits were completely finished.

    completely unsafe   completely safe

    C. Over 180,000 people gave it an average rating of 4.5 out of 5 stars on the Rotten Tomatoes movie review site.

    completely unsafe   completely safe

    D. Joe Morgenstern of the *Wall Street Journal* calls it "The best possible end for the series that began a decade ago."

    completely unsafe   completely safe

2. Claim: My parents should raise my allowance by $5 each week.

    Audience: Your parents or caregivers.

    A. All the kids in my class get more of an allowance than I do.

    completely unsafe   completely safe

B. The prices of the things I buy with my allowance have gone up.

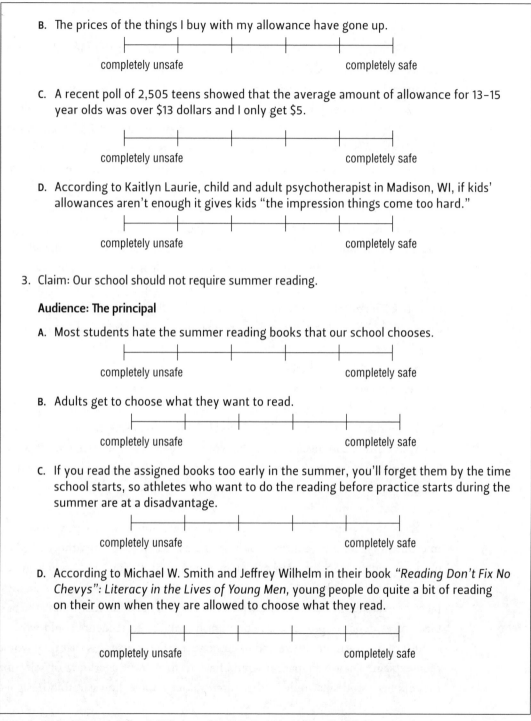

completely unsafe   completely safe

C. A recent poll of 2,505 teens showed that the average amount of allowance for 13–15 year olds was over $13 dollars and I only get $5.

completely unsafe   completely safe

D. According to Kaitlyn Laurie, child and adult psychotherapist in Madison, WI, if kids' allowances aren't enough it gives kids "the impression things come too hard."

completely unsafe   completely safe

3. Claim: Our school should not require summer reading.

Audience: The principal

A. Most students hate the summer reading books that our school chooses.

completely unsafe   completely safe

B. Adults get to choose what they want to read.

completely unsafe   completely safe

C. If you read the assigned books too early in the summer, you'll forget them by the time school starts, so athletes who want to do the reading before practice starts during the summer are at a disadvantage.

completely unsafe   completely safe

D. According to Michael W. Smith and Jeffrey Wilhelm in their book *"Reading Don't Fix No Chevys": Literacy in the Lives of Young Men,* young people do quite a bit of reading on their own when they are allowed to choose what they read.

completely unsafe   completely safe

the semantic differential scales will only be effective if at least some of the items are problematic.

Let's take a look at the items for claim C to share our thinking about what makes them problematic. In our work with schools we've found that it's a commonplace among students that summer reading is to be endured and not enjoyed. So the question is whether that commonplace is sufficiently well established to be able to proceed from. A discussion of the item might focus on the way it's phrased. For example, while some students would rate A as unsafe, they might rate this statement "Most students don't like the summer reading books that our school chooses as much as they like the books that they'd choose on their own" as much safer. On the surface, B seems to be simply an unsupported assertion, but when we test it against our experience we find it to be largely true. Students might argue that it's only true for pleasure reading or for adults who are no longer in school. Once again, the class could engage in profitable discussion about how to revise the statement to make it more likely to be accepted by the principal. The question in C, we think, is whether the principal would agree with three ideas: that athletes might want to read the books early; that if they do so, they'll forget them; and that forgetting them will be a disadvantage. All three seem to us to be on the edge of obvious but maybe not quite there. Of course, we'd expect everyone to acquiesce to the expertise of the educational researchers in D. But seriously, D raises some interesting questions. Is one study enough? Can you generalize from boys to all students? Is "quite a bit" specific enough to carry any weight? If the items in our model wouldn't work for your students, it would be easy to adjust the worksheet to feature claims your kids cared about. Replaying arguments you've heard from your students or the kids in your family would suggest both claims and evidence.

➤ *Lesson idea*   As a follow-up, you could give the class the same newspaper, magazine, Internet story, column, editorial, or blog and ask them to identify the single best piece of evidence. So, for example, say the initial text was on capital punishment. You could tell half the students in the class to read the text looking for the best piece of evidence in favor of capital punishment and the other half to find the best piece of evidence opposed to capital punishment. Then students could work in groups to discuss their choice and to come to a group consensus that they would then explain. Their explanation would have to focus on the criteria of selection they applied. Students would have to discuss, for example, how carefully designed a study must be in order to be generalized from, how expert an expert has to be in order to be trusted, how detailed a story has to be in order to be believed. Once again we see the interplay of declarative and procedural knowledge. Students are gaining both a declarative knowledge of the criteria and the procedural knowledge of how to apply them. As we noted in Chapter 3, they are developing strategies for what he calls "mining texts in reading to write" (Greene 1992).

➤ Writing anchor standards 1 and 8; speaking and listening anchor standards 1, 3, and 4

Thinking about targeting data to your audience. A great follow-up would be to track the story by looking at letters to the editor of comments on the blog to see what those who agreed with the initial text focused on and what those who didn't focused on.

➤ Lesson idea

Students' analysis of the letters or the comments would help them see the extent to which the audience determines what evidence is safe and what evidence is not, especially if the letters to the editor or comments identified the writer in one way or another. So too would returning to the items from the "Is It Safe?" worksheet and asking students to rank the items in the order that they think would be most effective for the named audience and then to rank them again for a different audience. So in item 1, would the ranking be the same for classmates and parents? Would they be the same in 2 for parents and for friends? In 3, would they be the same for the principal and for parents ?

➤ Writing anchor standard 1; speaking and listening anchor standards 1 and 4; reading anchor standards 5, 6, 8, and 9

Generating data. The mining texts activity that we described above is one way to help students understand how to generate data. It's a step on the way to helping students develop the procedural knowledge of substance they need to compose effective arguments and it is very much in line with the research strand of the CCSS that calls for students by grade 12 to be able to "gather relevant information from multiple authoritative print and digital sources." But the emphasis in the mining text activity is on the "gather[ing]" and the "relevant" and not on the "authoritative." Of course, texts vary in the likelihood that they will provide effective data, so students need to develop articulated understandings about how to employ search procedures.

➤ Writing anchor standard 8

One common way schools do this is simply to tell students what kind of sites they should go to and what sites they shouldn't. For example, like many high schools, the one Michael's daughters went to prohibited students from using Wikipedia as a site and instead encouraged them to use JSTOR. This is problematic for a number of reasons. First, it doesn't recognize that many middle and high school students will unlikely be able to read articles indexed in JSTOR without substantial background information of the sort they might be able to get from Wikipedia. Second, it ignores a crucial aspect of employing electronic databases: determining which search terms are most useful to use.

➤ *Lesson idea*

We suggest modeling how you would approach a search on a topic of interest, say, summer reading. You could explain if you'd start with Google, Google Scholar, JSTOR, ERIC, or somewhere else and why. You could talk about the search terms you'd use and how you might move from one to the next. Finally, we suggest having students work with the searches that you've done, identifying and ranking the first five sources they would go to from those identified by searching "pros and cons of summer reading in Google" and then doing the same for the sources identified by ERIC or some other database. Remember, simply telling kids what they should and shouldn't do is never enough. We have to engage them so that they can develop the procedural knowledge they will need.

If our goal is to prepare our students for college, however, we have to do more than have them write from texts. In many fields, and in many of the most immediate arguments students face, they'll have to supplement the published material that they find with other kinds of data, for example, by conducting interviews or doing surveys. Easier said than done, we've come to understand after years of doing our own research. Simply telling students to conduct an interview doesn't mean they can do so effectively. Once again, they'll need practice if they are to avoid the common pitfalls of asking either/or questions or indicating the kind of answer they are hoping to receive by the way they phrase their questions. A lesson

➤ *Lesson idea*

on interviewing doesn't have to be elaborate. It could begin by having students critique news reporters' questions (sports reporters are notorious). Then students could write questions to interview classmates on a topic of interest, say, the most important characteristics of a good teacher. Students could then interview each other and share the questions that worked and those that didn't. Then groups of students could work together to draft questions for people outside the class: other teachers, their parents, and so on, and conduct those interviews. Finally, the class could share the results of their interviews. Students could share the results of their interviews, by debriefing on both their method and the responses they elicited. They could discuss, for example, what qualities characterized good questions and whether good questions were good questions regardless of the interviewee or whether questions need to be tailored for the audience. They could also select the one or two most compelling pieces of evidence their respondents provided. Like the print texts we discussed above, interviews also have to be mined, so it's important to give students practice in doing so.

➤ *Writing anchor standard 7*

Warrants

For many students, the most difficult aspect of composing effective arguments is the warrant. That difficulty makes sense given that so many arguments proceed with unstated warrants, as we noted in our discussion of ads. To counter that state of affairs, we tried to put students in situations in which arguments hinged almost exclusively on providing warrants. Our friends and colleagues Betsy Kahn and Larry Johannessen helped us to see that one life situation that depends on warrants is comparison shopping. Think about the last time you were deciding which car to buy. The data were clear: you surely knew the price, EPA estimated mileage, and so on. Your choice depended on how you valued those data, that is, on the general rule that you applied to the purchase. Does fuel economy matter more than original purchase price? Does a longer warranty outweigh more interior bells and whistles? The answers to those questions are warrants.

We suggest an activity in which you cast your students as comparison shoppers. Each group of four could debate one product. You should select products that kids care about, like computer tablets, cell phones, or mp3 players. You should select two products that seem to you to be of similar quality and share information on them, from *Consumer Reports* or a comparison website. Then debaters would take turns speaking, for up to two minutes, on why to buy one product over another. After the debates, the audience could vote on a winner and explain their reasoning. Or they could diagram what they saw as the most and least effective arguments that they heard and discuss their choices. Whatever follow-up you choose, it's important to make sure that the audience, as well as the speakers, are benefiting from the activity.

➤ *Lesson idea*

➤ *Speaking and listening anchor standards 1, 2, 3, 4, and 6*

Trials are another arena in which evidence is often clear but in which the significance of the evidence is very much under dispute. Hillocks (2011) details how one could use minute mysteries to foster students' understanding of warrants. You've likely seen them in puzzle books. Minute mysteries present readers with a picture of a crime scene and a description of a situation. In order to

➤ *Lesson idea*

solve the crime students must carefully attend to the evidence in the picture and the scene. The data in the picture and in the description of the scene are, for the most part, not under dispute. Offering a persuasive solution to the crime depends on students' ability to explain how the evidence they noticed leads to the solution they offer, that is, on the warrants they provide.

Just as fictional crime scenes place an emphasis of warrants so do actual ones. Imagine the energy in a class that was considering the quality of the arguments in the Casey Anthony trial. Once again, the work we're suggesting not only helps students deepen their procedural and declarative knowledge, it also shows why what they're learning matters so much for their out-of-school lives.

You could also return to work students have already done and have them work together to write warrants for the evidence worksheet that we discussed above. The key, as we've argued throughout this book, is to make sure that students get enough practice.

Preparing for and Responding to Anticipated Arguments

Whereas students may not be used to composing warrants because warrants so often go unstated in everyday arguments, they are certainly used to tailoring arguments for the demands of different immediate situations. Michael and Jeff can attest to their own kids' knowing just which buttons to push to get what they want from their dads, and which entirely different buttons to push to manipulate their moms.

When students have tacit understandings to which you want to draw their attention, drama is always a good idea as Jeff has explained elsewhere (Wilhelm 1997/2008, 2002; Wilhelm and Edmiston 1998). We've suggested using drama previously, though we haven't labeled them as such, when we talked about casting students as detectives or comparison shoppers. Now we suggest developing dramatic situations a bit more fully. Here's one we've used with some success:

> Pretend that you and your classmates want to petition the principal of your school to increase his supervision of [Mr. Smith, Mr. Wilhelm, Mr. Fredricksen], your English teacher. Your primary concern is that you don't think your teacher does enough to help students learn. You know that last semester one

➤ Lesson idea

➤ Reading anchor standards 1, 3, and 8; speaking and listening anchor standards 1, 2, 3, and 4

➤ Lesson idea

student received an A, one student received a B, ten received
Cs, and ten received Ds or Fs. What do you think your principal
might say in response to your argument? What would you have
to do to overcome that response? Work in groups to develop a
strategy for overcoming the potential objections your principal
might have.

After students have discussed how they would have responded, we suggest
changing the scene a bit and talking with the class about other potential audiences
for the argument. For example, say that they were trying to convince their parents
to register a complaint against Mr. Smith, Mr. Wilhelm, or Mr. Fredricksen. What
might their parents say in response? How would that be different from what the
principal might say?

We realize that the kind of instruction we're calling for is much more
elaborate and will take much more time than the instruction that typifies
instruction in argumentation in most schools. As we noted earlier in this
chapter, however, this kind of elaborate preparation doesn't have to occur in
each grade. Perhaps some version of it in sixth grade and then again in ninth
grade with review along the way will suffice. If you save presenting instruction on developing original data through interviewing, surveys, and the like
until students will need to employ those techniques, you might want to use a
schedule something like the following:

- Week 1: Introducing Toulmin through talk, add analysis, production,
  and presentation.

- Week 2: PMI, Is It Safe?, activities on evaluating and mining source
  material.

- Week 3: Product debates, audience dramas.

We have to grant that providing this preparation and the follow-up we'll
discuss in the next chapter will mean that something that's currently in your
curriculum will have to go. But we think this kind of deep instruction is what the
CCSS are calling for. Remember, the CCSS include only ten standards for writing
and reading, and only six for language and speaking and listening, each playing
out somewhat differently moving from grades 6–12. But those few standards

are designed to place new and more rigorous demands on students. We have to prepare students to meet those demands. It'll take some time to do so.

We also realize that it's not easy to resist the press for coverage that so many teachers feel and to devote the time we're suggesting to help students understand and be able to produce effective arguments. But we think that the CCSS can help us advocate for the kind of instruction we're calling for. Teachers' lives have been made much more difficult in recent years by the standards movement. We should use those standards whenever we can as levers for progressive practice.

CHAPTER 6

Putting It Together in Simulations and Debates

I n the last chapter we talked at length about how to tap students' oral abilities to help them develop the knowledge needed to compose effective written arguments. That oral work was designed to help students develop articulated understandings of the elements of Toulmin's model. With the exception of the product debates, it was also largely conversational. The emphasis on conversation is designed to give students repeated exposure to the conversational prompts that cue the production of different elements of Toulmin's model.

If students are to write effectively, however, they have to be able to compose without the benefit of a conversational partner. Instead they have to internalize the prompts that a conversational partner would provide. Those conversational prompts, however, aren't enough because in oral argument each participant's responses are very short. Helping students produce extended arguments instead of short argumentative turns will require additional work.

An Argument for Simulations and Debates

Simulations and debates are a great way to bridge the gap between conversation and more extended compositions. In fact, Lynn Troyka's (1973) study of the effect of simulations had by far the largest effect size of any of the studies Hillocks (1986) reviewed in his comprehensive review of research on written composition. The instruction that Troyka studied involved engaging students in a series of problems, for example, a pollution problem and a neighborhood crime problem. In each problem the situation, roles, and rules for participation were specified. Students worked together with others who had a similar role (e.g., all of the homeowners in a simulation would work together) in small groups to plan how they would try to persuade other groups of their position in a series of public hearings.

Troyka's (1973) study provides compelling evidence of the power of more formal speaking opportunities, but it's a bit old and it involved college students. Therefore, we'd like to share in greater depth two wonderfully rich teacher-research studies that support her position.

Mary Beth Monahan (2001), an elementary school teacher who taught all the subject areas to her sixth graders, began her project because her students "produced arid prose—nearly voiceless essays that, at most, carried the muffled tones of resignation" (2). To work against that tendency, she embedded her writing instruction into a science unit in which students played the roles of "science sleuths" to provide a scientific explanation of a problem posed via video by a commercially available science program. The central question was why a company's frozen drinks weighed more than their liquid drinks even though the two products had the exact same ingredients in the exact same amounts.

In their roles as sleuths, students developed three distinct theories, which they debated with their fellow science sleuths and ultimately wrote about. Along the way, Mary Beth worked with her students to articulate the moves they were making as they developed their arguments, what she called an "essay tool box." She used Toulmin's terms, but her students also invented ones of their own that became part of the classroom lexicon such as "defend your shoot down" for what we called *responding to a rebuttal* in Chapter 2.

The primary purpose of Mary Beth's study was to examine her developing understanding of "voice," not to assess the effectiveness of her instruction. Nonetheless, the student writing that she shared strongly suggests that her instruction resulted in students taking a more authoritative stance in their writing. By the end of the project, her students portrayed themselves as makers of knowledge, as affiliated with others who also played the role of experts, and as confident responders to those who took different positions.

In fact, Mary Beth worried that the simulation resulted in her students being *too* authoritative. She thought that she portrayed argumentation as perhaps too agonistic and determined that she would tone down the militaristic rhetoric she found herself and her students employing (e.g., "shoot down the other side"). But as the conclusion of the paper of one of her students demonstrates, their writing was a far cry from the arid prose that so worried her when she began her work:

> "The crack is microscopic, so you need a microscope to see it." But how could this be? A microscopic crack would not let out any K!Zing!! If we now assume that the crack somehow did get by Kate and it leaked, the bottle would be lighter instead of heavier. To this Nick responded, "We are not saying that the frozen product is heavier, but that the liquid drink is getting lighter." Again you would fail. As you know, the original K!Zing! drinks were the correct weight, but the K!Zing! Kisicles were frozen and somewhere in that freezing process, the drink gained the minimal weight. And so I conclude my case.

Kristen Turner (2005), a high school teacher of both social studies and English, examined the impact of formal debate on students' argumentative writing in an American studies class she was coteaching with a colleague. She and her teaching partner embedded their work on argument early in a unit that focused on the essential question "What other voices have I not heard, and why?" Because they introduced the debate while they were considering how women's voices appeared or were silenced, the topics that she and her teaching partner chose had to do with issues of women's rights: "Should the Equal Rights Amendment (ERA) be adopted into the United States Constitution?" and "Should Title IX be amended?"

Kristen worked with her students to understand Toulmin's model in preparation for the debate and the writing they were going to do. Her introductory work was consistent with that which we describe in Chapter 4, though she delineated a variety of types of evidence (scientific laws, statistical, expert opinion, opinion of well-known individuals, and anecdotal evidence) that we did not discuss.

After this introductory work, students drew cards to find out what topic they would be working on and then began their research, which they used both to prepare for the debate and to write the first draft of an argumentative essay. Their research also provided valuable background information for their reading of the historical and literary texts they were discussing. During this time, Kristen offered whole-group instruction each day to prompt her students to develop claims, to consider counterarguments, to evaluate evidence based on a hierarchy, and to consider the warrant for each piece of evidence.

In the debates themselves, as the chart below indicates, each team had four members who would speak for 2–5 minutes, depending on their role:

Speaker	Job	Minutes
PRO 1	State the proposition for the team; introduce the arguments and present evidence in support of them	3–5
CON Q	Poke holes in the PRO argument by asking questions; do not offer exposition	2
CON 1	Counter the proposition; introduce CON arguments while beginning to attack PRO position	3–5
PRO Q	Poke holes in the CON argument by asking questions; do not offer exposition	2
PRO 2	Rebuild the PRO argument and address the CON position	3–5
CON Q	Poke holes in the PRO argument by asking questions; do not offer exposition	2
CON 2	Rebuild the CON argument and address the PRO position	3–5
PRO Q	Poke holes in the CON argument by asking questions; do not offer exposition	2
CON R	Summarize the debate while building the CON argument and attacking the PRO; do not add any new information	2
PRO R	Summarize the debate while building the PRO argument and attacking the CON; do not add any new information	2

Kristen found that the instruction on debate worked well to improve students' attention to supporting their claims with effective data and especially to anticipating and responding to potential objections. The revised papers students completed after the debate were much stronger than the initial drafts. Moreover, two thirds of the focal students in her study came out of the unit with a much deeper understanding of writing arguments. Here's how one of them put it:

> I had like an epiphany, everything's like an argument now. Anything can be an argument. Just by looking at this stuff. 'Cause like I said before about the personal review, when I write for another class, I don't feel it's the same. But now, I realize that it really is. I mean, argument, if I'm talking about something in class, in lit class, like when we were talking about minorities or women, whatever, if I have a point, that's my argument, and I say how I'm supporting that. And if we happen to be talking about something in another, a different class, and it's something similar to that or something about something we have learned, like a topic or whatever, and I have a question about that or have a feeling about that, that's, like, I have an argument about, you know what I mean? So, it really can be applied to anything.

Unfortunately, Kristen's study also establishes that this kind of transfer is difficult to achieve, which makes sense given the extent to which arguments are context dependent, a point that we explored in Chapter 3. Although her students appeared to transfer what they learned about evidence into the literary analyses she asked them to write after the debate, they were not as successful in transferring what they seemed to have learned about claims and, especially, about rebuttals. It seems that they regarded their literary analyses more as performances for the teacher than as arguments that sought to establish a claim or set of claims from among possibly competing claims. As Kristen notes, cultivating what Haskell (2001) calls a "spirit of transfer" and "cultures of transfer" (46) takes some doing. (We'll be exploring ways of doing that cultivation in the next chapter.)

Both Mary Beth's and Kristen's work suggests that simulations and debates, oral work that's more extended and hence more writing-like than conversation, can be powerful tools in helping students bring what they already can do orally to their writing. But we think it's important to note that debates and simulations are important also for helping students develop their speaking and listening abilities. In our experience, teachers talk about teaching reading, writing, speaking, listening, and (sometimes) viewing. However, for most people (ourselves included) reading and writing rule the roost. Simulations and debates are great ways to bring the language arts into better balance in our classrooms. They are a great way to work toward the CCSS' standards on speaking and listening, especially the call to prepare students to "present information, findings, and supporting evidence such that listeners can follow the line of reasoning and the organization, development, and style are appropriate to task, purpose, and audience" and to "adapt speech to a variety of contexts and communicative tasks, demonstrating command of formal English when indicated or appropriate."

➤ *Speaking and listening anchor standards 4 and 6*

Thinking About Planning

Okay, we know what you may be thinking: "All that preparatory work they talked about in Chapter 5 and now this! I can't fit any more into my schedule. We have too much reading to do." We also know that all three examples we cited come from a context different from most teachers'. Lynn Troyka's (1973) study was in a college composition class. The fact that Mary Beth Monahan taught all subjects to her students allowed her to use science as the disciplinary context for the teaching of argument so she didn't have to give up any reading to do it. Kristen Turner team-taught American studies with a social studies teacher. The policy debates clearly fit into social studies, though Kristen did them in her English classes as well.

We should also add a confession. When Michael, the lead author for this book, taught, his school divided first-year English into a semester that focused on teaching writing and a semester that focused on the teaching of reading and literature because the school wanted to make sure that students received substantial instruction in the teaching of writing. Michael's thinking about the teaching of argumentative writing, then, was formed in a context in which he didn't have to give up reading any literature in order to do it.

So let's think about planning for simulations and debates in a more typical English classroom. Let's imagine that we're teaching the grade to which the bulk of the preliminary teaching that we discussed last chapter has been assigned. As we noted there, if you did the lessons we suggested consecutively, it would take about three weeks if you didn't do extended work in helping students understand how to develop interview or survey questions. Let's imagine further that you're planning to teach the question that we talked about in Chapter 4: "To what extent are people responsible for what happens to them?"

Step 1: Identify a Public Policy Issue Related to the Inquiry Unit You're Working On

Knowing where your students will be going lets you plan simulations and debates that do double-duty. Myriad school and public policy issues relate to the essential question, so the work that students do discussing the issues provides a conceptual framework for the reading they'll be doing. And much of that reading will be of the kind of explanatory and informational texts the CCSS call for.

➤ *Reading anchor standards 1, 2, 8, 9, and 10*

You might remember that we suggested introducing that question by having students consider two cases that had to do with hazing and bullying. One possible relevant topic, then, could be something like "The school should do more to protect students from bullying."

➤ *Lesson idea*

Or you could have students work on a public policy issue more directly related to *Romeo and Juliet*, one of the texts we suggested as appropriate for the essential question. As a quick online search will reveal, almost every state has some kind of law that holds parents responsible for the wrongdoing of their unemancipated children. You could have students do a simulation or debate on those laws.

➤ *Lesson idea*

Another possibility would be to have students examine bans on violent video games or the censoring of misogynistic lyrics. Both turn on the extent to which outside forces can be held responsible to an individual's choices. So too do lawsuits that seek to hold fast-food restaurants responsible for childhood obesity. So too do discussions of the social safety net. Our point is simply this: Once you've articulated an essential question, you'll have a wide variety of possible school or public policy issues from which to choose.

➤ *Lesson idea*

Step 2: Determine Whether a Simulation or Debate Would Better Meet Your Goals and Share the Rules of Engagement

The next step is to decide whether you want to have students do a simulation or a debate. A simulation depends on specifying a real-world context in which the

➤ *Lesson idea*

discussion of a policy could take place. For example, the bullying policy could be discussed at a student council or school board meeting. It would be great if you could arrange for students to present their cases in front of an actual audience of policy makers. For instance, as part of their work in a unit built around the question, "On balance, have sports had a positive or negative effect on American society?," a group of Jeff's students presented an argument in front of the school board, arguing that the school should uncouple homecoming from football and make it about all fall activities. If you can't arrange for an actual audience, then you or some of your students will have to play the role of those policy makers. Once you've determined the context, it's crucial to specify the rules of participation. One problematic aspect of simulations is making sure that a few students don't dominate. One advantage of debates is that the format necessitates nearly equal participation. But doing a series of debates might take longer than a single simulation and students don't get to borrow the authority of their roles when they develop their arguments. If you do a simulation, you should play a role too. For example, you could play the student council president or the school board president and conduct the meeting in role.

➤ *Speaking and listening anchor standard 3*

Regardless of whether you do a simulation or a debate, the next step is to work with students to understand who would be affected by the issue. In the case of bullying, bullied students, bullies, unaffected students, parents, teachers, school staff, and school administrators come immediately to mind. If you do a simulation, students should make their case from the perspective of their roles. If you do a debate, they should be aware of who might be affected by the policies they are discussing.

Step 3: Work with Students as They Develop Their Cases

➤ *Lesson idea*

The next step is to work with students to develop their cases. Some topics might require original research. For example, in preparing to discuss the bullying topic students might want to do some kind of survey to assess the magnitude of the problem. You also have to think through how you want to scaffold the research students need to do. One way to do so is to make use of sourcebooks on the national high school debate topic, which always centers on an important public policy issue. Each year a variety of companies create compendiums of discrete pieces of evidence from a wide range of sources that speak to the topic. One way to scaffold students' participation would be to give them access to some portion of one of these books. Students wouldn't have to find their own evidence, but they would have to understand the evidence that's presented in the sourcebook.

This work is helping them meet the text complexity standard of the CCSS. To be sure, much literature commonly taught in schools is very difficult. We have argued (Smith and Wilhelm 2002) that some of it is too hard, in fact. But we also need to understand that narrative structure supports students' understanding. Indeed Graesser, McNamara, and Kulikowich (2011) have found that the relative proportion of narrativity and the complexity of syntax were the most significant correlates to text difficulty. As the CCSS point out, if we want to prepare our students for college, we have to prepare them to read the difficult disciplinary essays they'll encounter there, essays that may include some narrative elements but that are dominated by text structures that are nonnarrative.

Simulations and debates that are part of inquiry units provide wonderful opportunities to give students supported experience with the difficult informational texts they are likely to encounter in the sciences and the social sciences. Because students will be reading the texts as part of a unit of study, their content knowledge will help support their reading. If you employ sourcebooks, students will only have to read very short, self-contained texts, which will allow them to work to understand the difficult syntax without major demands on their memory. In short, simulations and debates that are part of inquiry units create a context in which students are motivated to read, understand, and use complex nonnarrative texts.

➤ *Reading anchor standards 1, 2, 8, 9, and 10*

Steps 4–6: Run the Simulation or Debate, Debrief About What Arguments Were Successful and What Arguments Weren't, and Have Students Write or Revise on the Basis of What They've Learned

After the simulation or the debate, we suggest talking in small groups and as a class about which arguments worked and why and which ones didn't and why. Then students could write about the policy, either from the perspective of the role they played or from their own perspective. Or, if you followed Kristen Turner's lead and had them write a first draft before the debate or simulation, they could write a revision after the oral activity. Comparing the two papers can teach students a lot about what they can accomplish through revision.

➤ *Writing anchor standards 1, 4, 5, and 10*

Developing Simulations and Debates in Inquiry Units

- Identify a public policy issue related to the inquiry unit you're working on.

- Determine whether a simulation or debate would better meet your goals and share the rules of engagement.

- Work with students as they develop their cases.

- Run the simulation or debate.

- Debrief about what arguments were successful and what arguments weren't.

- Have students write or revise on the basis of what they've learned.

So let's put it all together and sketch out a unit calendar:

- Week 1: Introducing Toulmin through talk, add analysis, production, and presentation.

- Week 2: PMI, Is It Safe, exercises on evaluating and mining source material.

- Week 3: Product debates, audience dramas.

- Week 4: Introducing the essential question, examining it through current events and a short literary text, begin research on an issue that will be explored in a simulation.

- Week 5: Write draft of paper assigning responsibility for that issue, simulation, revise draft based on simulation.

- Weeks 6–? Continue exploration of essential question through other texts, activities, and writing.

In our next chapter we'll turn to discussing teaching a variety of kinds of arguments related to literature. But before we do, we want to stress again the importance of making sure our students get the practice they need to develop the procedural, declarative, and contextual knowledge they need to compose arguments. Simulations and debates require students to put the knowledge they have developed into practice in a meaningful and motivating context.

CHAPTER 7

Teaching Argument Through the Study of Literature and Reading

I n Chapter 4, we noted that arguments were absent in many English language arts classrooms and attributed that absence to the tendency for teachers, even those who wish to foster lively conversational exchanges, to feel pressure to move their classes to a common understanding of what's being read (cf. Marshall, Smagorinsky, and Smith 1995). This tendency, we think, is in large measure a legacy of the New Criticism, the theoretical foundation for much of the teaching of literature in secondary schools, the fundamental premise of which is that a work of literature is a self-contained entity whose meaning can be objectively understood. A countervailing theory that's becoming more commonly enacted in schools is reader-response theory. Although there are many very different varieties of reader response, most share the belief that meaning does not inhere in a text but rather *in* a reader or *in the reader's transaction* with the text. This theory would also seem to mitigate against argument, for a reader could say something like, "Well, that's what it means to me," rather than develop an interpretive argument.

We don't want to get embroiled in a long theoretical debate (you can see Michael's thinking on the issue in *Authorizing Readers* [Rabinowitz and Smith 1998]). But it's worth noting that there are pressures that work against making argument central to the work we do when we teach literature and reading. The purpose of this chapter is to try to overcome those pressures by explaining four different kinds of arguments relevant to the teaching of literature and reading: interpretive arguments about a single text, judgments about characters and their actions, arguments about ideas, and evaluative arguments. You may not want to use all of them depending on your theoretical perspective, but all of them would, we think, help you work to achieve the CCSS.

Interpretive Analyses of Individual Texts

By *literary analyses* we mean compositions that focus on answering at least the first half of what Michael and Peter Rabinowitz (1998) call the authorial reading question: "What would this mean for the audience the author was writing for and how do I feel about that?" (They contrast that question with what they call the New Critical question's "What does this mean?" and the reader-response question's "What does this mean to me?") Sounds kind of old-fashioned, we know, but we don't think it is. Michael and Peter argue for the theoretical, ethical, and pedagogical benefits of asking such a question. But we don't think you need to run out and buy the book to be convinced (though Michael would be delighted if you did). We think that your experience as a reader will reveal the generative nature of the question.

Our experiences do. Michael and Jeff are in book clubs and their best discussions are always informed, at least in part, by asking that question. For example, Michael's club had a very rich discussion about how Jonathan Franzen wants his readers to feel about Walter Berglund, one of the main characters in *Freedom*. To what extent does he want Walter's obsession with the safety of birds to be admired? How does he want his audience to feel about Walter's affair with Lalitha? What did Franzen hope to accomplish by killing Lalitha off so soon after the affair was consummated?

Jeff's book club just finished reading *Desert* by the Nobel laureate J. M. Clotzier. Several energetic exchanges at their meeting revolved around what the group thought Clotzier wanted them to think about nature, particularly the desert, about native groups versus colonial cultures, and how they were to regard L's journey to Marseille and her return to Morocco to have her baby.

Jim's not in a book club, but Jeff's and Michael's experience resonate with him. In the hallway of his English department Jim and a few colleagues started talking about *Catch-22* and the story NPR did on the fiftieth anniversary of its publication. What did Joseph Heller want his readers to understand about Yossarian? How did the character of Yossarian change from the audience in 1961 through the rest of the Vietnam War? What was Heller trying to say through Yossarian's understanding of war and through the tone?

If you agree that interpretive arguments are both important and energizing, then you will want your students to write them. But if you were persuaded by our discussion of the five kinds of knowledge in Chapter 3, you'll realize that students need more than even the deepest understanding of the text about which they are writing (declarative knowledge of substance). They'll need more than even the most highly specified assignment and rubric (declarative knowledge of form). You'll need to help them develop procedural knowledge of both form and substance. And you'll need to set up a context in which arguments matter.

Remember when we talked about the comparison shopping in Chapter 5 ? We explained that different kinds of arguments place different emphases on different elements of argument. If we want to help our students develop the procedural knowledge that they will need, we have to begin by understanding the demands that literary analyses place on writers.

Claims

Literary analyses seem to place special emphasis on making a defensible yet debatable claim. Claims in policy arguments are relatively easy. If you paid any attention at all during the debate on health care, you know that a key issue was whether the proposal should have a single-payer option. A claim flows easily from that recognition. If your school is like ours, there are issues swirling around on which a variety of positions have been identified and staked out. In thinking about summer reading, for example, you have to decide whether your school should require common summer reading, should require reading but allow some kind of choice, or should not require summer reading at all. The choice option has a variety of possible permutations, but, for the most part, the claims one could make on the issue are readily identifiable. But now think about an interpretive composition on a literary text. So many possibilities!

And so many chances to go astray, especially by choosing to write about an inauthentic question. How does Browning want readers to feel about the speaker of "My Last Duchess"? No argument there; how could anyone see him as other than a murderous brute? What characters are symbolized by mockingbirds in *To Kill a Mockingbird*? Tom and Boo. A writer could provide plenty of evidence to justify that interpretation, but it wouldn't be worth doing. No one could think otherwise. How does Steinbeck want readers to feel about George's killing of Lennie in *Of Mice and Men*? The whole story of Crooks' dog is clearly designed to endorse George's choice.

We chose canonical literary texts for our examples in the hope that most of our readers would be acquainted with at least one of them. But our point isn't limited to canonical texts. Interpretive arguments are only worth making if alternative interpretations are plausible. Therefore, it seems to us that teaching interpretive arguments requires creating a classroom context that encourages alternative interpretations.

One way to do so is to regularly teach texts that have alternative interpretations and to reserve asking students to compose literary analyses for those texts—being mindful of the fact that there are lots of other kinds of arguments related to literature that students can compose. So, for example, one strand of an inquiry unit built around the question "To what extent can people understand each other across demographic differences?" would likely focus on generational differences. As part of that strand we might well choose to teach two poems about sons' relationships with their fathers: "Those Winter Sundays" by Robert Hayden and "My Papa's Waltz" by Theodore Roethke. We love both poems. But it seems to us that the range of interpretations of "Those Winter Sundays" is far more limited than is the range of interpretations for "My Papa's Waltz." "Those Winter Sundays" closes with a question: "What did I know, what did I know / of love's austere and lonely offices?" The answer seems clear to us: "Not much. Or at least not enough." On the other hand, you can be sure that your students will have different takes on the relationship between the father and son in "My Papa's Waltz" and the extent to which it's changed from the time of the action of the poem to the occasion upon which it's written.

A second way to encourage alternative interpretations, we think, is to deliberately try to change the nature of classroom discussion. Remember the research we reported in Chapter 4 about how rare open discussion is? One reason might be that teachers think of themselves as question askers rather than as problem posers. Our preservice teachers, anyway, often see planning a lesson on a text as developing a series of questions specific to that text.

Asking a series of text-specific questions is problematic for a number of reasons, the most significant of which is that in asking a question, the teacher or book has done much of the interpretive work by noticing what aspects of the text are worth asking about. Peter Rabinowitz (cf., Rabinowitz 1987; Rabinowitz and Smith 1998) has convinced us that such noticing is absolutely central to interpretation. That means that we have to try to help students learn how to notice what's worth asking about on their own. Being able to recognize what's worth attending to is at the heart of procedural knowledge of substance. Those are the details that will make up much of the composing students do.

If we want our students' procedural knowledge of substance to be robust, that is, if we want them to be able to apply what they learn from reading one story to their reading of the next, *they* have to be the ones to do the noticing. To do this, they need to understand the general cues authors depend upon them to notice and use to interpret character. If we ask questions about a text, it must be in service of helping the students to begin noticing the same cues and asking the same kinds of interpretive questions for themselves.

We don't want to go too far afield here. A complete examination of classroom discussion could be a book in itself (we refer you to the brilliant *Talking in Class: Using Discussion to Enhance Teaching and Learning* [McCann, Johannessen, Kahn, and Flanagan 2006]) and we've written about this idea elsewhere (Smith and Wilhelm 2010), but let's just take one example. One of the things that readers have to do as they read any text is separate the wheat from the chaff—that is, to pay attention to that which is most important. So we suggest regularly posing the problem "What's the most important word (for a poem), or character or scene?" Try the most important word problem with "Those Winter Sundays." Michael thinks the answer is *too*. Jeff thinks it's *know*. Jim chimes in with *thanked*.

> ➤ *Lesson idea*
> ➤ *Reading anchor standards 4 and 5*

Another way to encourage alternative interpretations is to at least occasionally read a text with them that you've never read before. That way you can't have prepared answers for the questions you pose. It's easy enough to do, regardless of the unit inquiry you're pursuing. You just have to tell a colleague the inquiry you're working on and ask him or her to bring in a class set of copies of a text. Michael and Bill Connolly (2003), a teacher who took the risk of doing first-time reading along with his students, studied the effect of doing so and found, interestingly, that both the students and Bill himself felt freer to talk and to disagree. Here's what one student said: "It made him more like 'one of us,' that is, we were not hearing responses from someone who knew the poem like the back of his hand." And another:

> ➤ *Lesson idea*

> Whatever came to mind, I wrote [in my journal]. There was nothing holding me back. The teacher had not read the poem before, so he was doing the same thing as me—trying to understand it.

Here are a couple of entries from Bill's teaching journal:

> I like how I felt comfortable not knowing it all and equally comfortable giving my opinion or interpretation.

> I have to say that I feel there was respect for my authority (as teacher) but a number of kids had no qualms about disagreeing with me. . . . I feel good about that type of authority. My kids feel comfortable disagreeing with me.

Our point is simply this: Working with students to write literary analyses depends on creating a context in which a variety of interpretations are possible. Students need to be able to employ the PMI when they write their literary analyses as much as when they write about policy issues.

Data

One of the major differences between literary analyses and other kinds of arguments is that in literary analyses the primary source of data is absolutely obvious: the piece of literature. But that doesn't mean we don't have to help students develop procedural knowledge of substance. As we argued above, the key is helping students understand the rules of notice we apply as experienced readers. That is, we need to be able to help them mine literary texts in much the same way as we helped them think about mining nonliterary texts in Chapter 5. Peter Rabinowitz's *Before Reading* (1987, also available online) is a wonderfully rich account of why we notice what we notice, and we encourage you to take a look at it. But it's easy enough to start a catalog on your own and with your students. Why do we pay attention to mockingbirds in *To Kill a Mockingbird*? The title, of course. We privilege beginnings and endings. Repetition and patterns make us take notice. Undue attention to seemingly insignificant details warrants our consideration. Lesley Rex and David McEachen coauthored an article titled "'If Anything Is Odd, Inappropriate, Confusing, or Boring, It's Probably Important': The Emergence of Inclusive Academic Literacy Through English Classroom Discussion Practices" (1999) that chronicles McEachen's work to integrate regular track students into a class for gifted and talented students. The title of the article is a rule of notice, and what McEachen tried to do was help his new students understand and apply it.

So one key aspect of helping students write literary analyses is to help them develop conscious control over principles of evidence selection. Think-alouds are one great way to do so (see Wilhelm 2001). In a think-aloud you simply say out loud everything you think as you read. If you do think-alouds in your classes, we strongly encourage you to do so with texts you haven't read before. Noticing in rereadings is very different from noticing in first readings.

➤ *Lesson idea*

Another key is to regularly have students reflect and share how they know what they know about a text. So, for example, after doing a "most important word" problem, you could ask students to write about why they selected what they selected. One way to share understandings is for the class to collaborate on a compilation of rules of reading in a children's book, say, or in an instruction manual that they could then share with an actual audience of younger students for whom they could be reading mentors. Because these rules work across texts, such work is composing to transfer.

➤ *Lesson idea*
➤ *Writing anchor standards 6 and 7*

Warrants

Many of the rules of reading that we just talked about can act as warrants to interpretive arguments. For example, we notice things that are patterned and so can explain an interpretation of some aspect of a text by illustrating how it fits in with a pattern. As David McEachen teaches his students, we notice departures from what is typical or expected. Ironically, one way to explicate these textual ruptures is to argue that while they seem surprising if they are understood in a particular way, they are in fact consistent with the rest of the text. So working with students to articulate the "rules of reading" does double-duty.

Another warrant often deployed in interpretive arguments is to reason about what an author intended something to mean by positing how he or she would have made different choices if he or she wanted to imply a different meaning. We suggest using art as a way to give students practice in employing this warrant.

➤ *Lesson idea*

One of Michael's favorite portraits is Velázquez's *A Dwarf Sitting on the Floor* (c. 1645), thought to be of Don Sebastián de Morra (Figure 7.1). The question "How does Velázquez want us to feel about the dwarf?" is a complex one that's sure to generate differences of opinions. You can prompt students to produce a warrant for their opinions that cites Velázquez's artistic choices by once again using the same questions you used to introduce Toulmin's model as in the following:

Figure 7.1   *The Dwarf Sebastián de Morra* by Diego Velázquez, c. 1645

S1: He wants us to feel sorry for him.

T: What makes you say so?

S1: He's sitting.

T: So what?

S1: Well, most portraits don't have people sitting.

T: So what?

S2: Well he could have pictured him just from the chest up like they usually do. That way we wouldn't even have known he was a dwarf. Or even if he were standing. His feet and legs wouldn't be right out front like that.

This is the aha moment. It might not happen right away, but we promise that it will happen. When it does, you should draw students' attention to it: "So you're understanding what Velázquez wants us to think by imagining how he would have done things differently if he had wanted us to think something else."

But the discussion won't end there, so you'll have the opportunity to prompt other students to produce this warrant:

S3: No you have it wrong. Look at his eyes.

T: What about his eyes?

S3: Well he's looking right at the audience. He's not hiding at all.

T: So what?

S3: If Velázquez had wanted us to feel sorry for him he would have had him looking away or hiding his eyes. People who look straight at you are powerful people. I think Velázquez wants us to see him as strong. Strong-willed anyway.

The conversation could (and would) continue. And it doesn't matter what understanding students ultimately have of the portrait. What does matter is that they've learned a very sophisticated move for making interpretive arguments that they can employ in writing about many different texts.

In order to cement that understanding, we suggest having whole-class or small-group discussions of a series of visual texts selected because they allow multiple interpretations. Those discussions will provide the opportunity to compose to practice. Because students get a chance to hear a range of interpretations, those discussions would help them develop knowledge of context and purpose. That is, the discussions would require students to think, Okay, what kind of argument do I have to make given the range of understandings my classmates revealed? Listing the differing views that emerged in class engages them in composing to plan. Students could then choose a single work and write a paper on it, requiring first draft and final draft composing.

Using visual texts is an especially good way to help students develop interpretive skills because students can get so much practice so quickly. You might be able to discuss four or more photographic or fine art portraits in a single block. Discussing written texts takes much longer, and the longer the text, the less practice students get transferring knowledge to new interpretive situations.

Another effective and efficient way to help students infer what the artistic choices made by the creator of a text imply is to look at multiple film versions of the same texts. For example, if you used *Romeo and Juliet* as one of the literary texts in a unit built on the question "To what extent are people responsible for what happens to them?" you could have the class watch the death of Mercutio in both the Zeffirelli and Luhrmann versions, identify the differences, and discuss what those differences suggest about the director's position on the essential question.

➤ *Lesson idea*

But moving to written texts is essential. When you do so, we suggest setting up routines that require students to apply the procedural knowledge they've developed. Although we worry about overreliance on story-specific questions, we think that questions that work across texts are very powerful. For example, whenever students read a story or part of a novel, you could ask them to do something like the following: "Select one (or two or three or four, depending on your students) thing(s) that you thought was especially important to notice and explain why you noticed it." Or, "Select what you see as the scene in the book that most clearly supports your understanding of a character or of an important idea the author is trying to communicate. Think about how that scene would have been different had the author been trying to communicate something different." That writing becomes composing to plan when students use what they and their classmates have written to do first and final draft composing of interpretive essays in which they explain their thinking on an interpretive problem the class has investigated but that is still under dispute.

➤ *Lesson idea*

➤ *Writing anchor standards 1, 4, 5, and 9; reading anchor standards 4 and 5*

Let's take a look at the CCSS and see how we're doing so far. The assignments and instruction we've discussed are clearly designed to meet writing standard 1: "Writing arguments to support claims with clear reasons and relevant evidence." As they work on their interpretive arguments, and get feedback about them from both the classmates and teachers, they are working on both rough draft and final draft composing and address both writing anchor standard 4 ("Produce clear and coherent writing in which the development, organization, and style are appropriate to task, purpose, and audience") and writing anchor standard 5 ("Develop and strengthen writing as needed by planning, revising, editing, rewriting, or trying a new approach").

They also meet at least some of writing anchor standard 9: "Draw evidence from literary or informational texts to support analyses, reflection, and research." But not all of it. We haven't addressed nonfiction texts at all and while the activities should help students research particular texts by making them more attuned to rules of notice, we don't think that that's the kind of research the CCSS is calling for. If we want to help our students meet the CCSS we have to do more than help them write interpretive essays on individual texts. We have to create contexts that put texts into meaningful conversation.

The activities also work to achieve the CCSS reading anchor standards, especially 4 and 5, two standards that relate to craft and structure:

4. Interpret words and phrases as they are used in a text,
    including determining technical, connotative, and figurative

meanings, and analyze how specific word choices shape meaning or tone.

5. Analyze the structure of texts, including how specific sentences, paragraphs, and larger portions of the text [(e.g., a section, chapter, scene, or stanza) relate to each other and the whole].

Making Judgments About Characters and Their Actions

As we've written elsewhere (Smith and Wilhelm 2010) we were drawn to this profession in large measure because of our love of literature and our recognition that literary characters have been critically important to us as we negotiate our lives. One of our favorite quotes comes from Wayne Booth (1988) in his wonderful book *The Company We Keep.* Booth notes that stories typically center on the characters' efforts to face moral choices and argues that "In tracing those efforts, we readers stretch our own capacities for thinking about how life should be lived" (187). Another longtime favorite comes from Robert Coles (1989) who shares what one of his students said about the importance of literary characters in his life:

> When I have some big moral issue, some question to tackle, I think I try to remember what my folks have said, or I imagine them in my situation—or even more these days I think of [characters in books I've read]. Those folks, they're people for me . . . they really speak to me—there's a lot of me in them, or vice versa. I don't know how to put it, but they're voices, and they help me make choices. I hope when I decide "the big ones" they'll be in there pitching. (203)

In Chapter 4 we discussed the importance of creating a context that rewards argumentation and argued that inquiry units built around essential questions are an extremely powerful way to do just that. A variety of essential questions focus on character. Some have to do with roles people play in their lives, such as "What makes a good friend? A good teacher? A good leader? A hero?" These questions can become more complex by asking the extent to which the answer depends on time, place, gender, or cultural group. Other character-based essential questions focus on personal qualities, such as "What makes a person resilient? What is loyalty? What is courage?" Again, the list could go on.

All of these questions are contested in our culture, so investigating any of them requires students to make and evaluate arguments. But we'd like to illustrate the approach we're advocating with an extended focus on just one, "What makes a person resilient?," a question Michael worked on with Olufemi Fadeyibi, one of his former students who teaches in the School District of Philadelphia. Olufemi determined the focus of his inquiry because he wanted to teach Walter Dean Myers' *The Beast*, a book that chronicles the relationship between a young man from Harlem who leaves his neighborhood to go to a private school as a way to improve life chances and his girlfriend, a young woman who had been successful in school but who becomes addicted to drugs. The book closes with the young woman's being released from a rehabilitation center, leaving her future unspeci-fied. The question that Myers seems to be posing at the end of the book is whether she has turned her life around or whether she'll return to the clutches of her addiction. In Olufemi and Michael's conversations about the book, Michael noted that he often thinks about potential turning points and wonders why some people seem to change and some don't. "Why is it," Michael asked, "that some people are resilient while others aren't?" Because Olufemi's students live in difficult circum-stances in a dangerous neighborhood, he thought that that question would be a useful one for them to consider.

This question relates to literature but it is a psychological one rather than a literary one. That means that in order for students to think about it responsibly, they have to employ psychological research. Olufemi did not want to overwhelm his students, so he and Michael did some Internet research to see what is known about resilience, ultimately drawing on Johnson and Howard's "Young Adoles-cents Displaying Resilient and Non-Resilient Behaviour: Insights from a Qualita-tive Study—Can Schools Make a Difference?" (2000, available online) to develop the chart displayed in Figure 7.2. This chart provides a wide range of possible warrants for an argument about someone's resilience. And in so doing, it provides a unit-specific rule of notice. That is, whenever we read a text for the purpose of thinking about an essential question, we pay special attention to any details that relate to that essential question. The discussion of the factors that foster resilience makes students notice those details as they read.

Figure 7.2 Factors That Lead to Resilience

LIFE EVENTS	SELF	FAMILY	SCHOOL	COMMUNITY
Life Circumstances ___ Healthy at birth ___ Continued good health ___ Opportunities to move ahead in life ___ Meeting important people ___ Moving into a more supportive community	**Personal Attributes** ___ The person is easygoing ___ The person is intelligent ___ The person is emotionally strong ___ The person is physically strong ___ The person is able to handle situations alone ___ The person has a sense of humor ___ The person gets along well with others **How a person handles life** ___ The person has strong problem-solving skills ___ The person is hopeful ___ The person thinks about life in a deep way **What the person believes about himself or herself** ___ The person has a positive self-image ___ The person believes he or she can get a job done	**Love and attachment** ___ Good relationship with parents ___ Good relationship with siblings ___ Good relationship with extended family **Support** ___ Has financial support—has enough money ___ Has emotional support **Parenting practices** ___ Parents are always available ___ Parents are nice ___ Parents have high expectations **Role models of resiliency** ___ Parents have made it ___ Siblings have made it ___ Extended family has made it	**Peer Interaction** ___ Has friends who stay out of trouble ___ Sees other students set high goals and expectations for themselves **School climate** ___ People work together ___ Teachers are caring ___ School is safe **Curriculum (school work that is assigned)** ___ What is learned can be used in different areas of life ___ Work is challenging ___ Necessary support is provided	**Adults** ___ Adults are successful ___ Adults are supportive ___ Adults are culturally proud **Peer** ___ Peers are successful ___ Peers are supportive ___ Peers have common interests ___ Peers are connected to the community **Institutions** ___ Community provides plenty to do ___ Community provides opportunities for success

➤ *Lesson idea*

In order to engage students in experiencing why the issue is important, Olufemi and Michael asked students to apply it to the life of a celebrity with whom students were familiar, the rapper Lil Wayne, who has had a number of brushes with the law and who was recently released from jail. They shared a brief summary of Lil Wayne's life and asked students to use the chart to argue whether he was on the road to recovery or ruin. Of course, Lil Wayne isn't the only celebrity one could use. Lindsay Lohan or Michael Vick or any of a host of others would work as well. But whomever you choose needs to be someone who could go either way. If everyone in the class makes the same judgment, the case is not complex enough to require students to think deeply to justify their arguments.

This kind of discussion is composing to practice as students have to construct complete arguments drawing on all the elements of Toulmin's model. Figure 7.3 provides the bio that they used and Figure 7.4 provides the planning sheet Olufemi provided.

➤ *Lesson idea*

Then Olufemi had students respond to a series of simulated texts (Figure 7.5). We draw on Judith Langer's (2001) research for the term. Langer defines simulated instruction as using texts and tasks specifically designed to focus students' attention to a particular learning outcome. In her words, simulated instruction involves employing "tasks . . . [that] are especially developed for the purpose of practice" (856). She argues that providing such instruction is one characteristic of teachers whose students beat the odds, that is, teachers whose students perform better on high-stakes assessments than their SES would predict. In our terms, a simulated text is one that a teacher would develop to provide that instruction.

The simulated texts forced the students to think hard about the resiliency table, as they are complex cases. Mikey, for example, has a good relationship with his father, but his father doesn't seem to have high expectations. He had good grades in the past but doesn't have them in the present. Most of his teachers have given up on him, but one hasn't. As a consequence, each case provides content for an authentic argument. During those arguments, Olufemi probed students to develop their ideas by using the "What makes you say so?," "So what?," and "How do you know?" prompts. He also pushed them to articulate the kind of details they would be looking for if the texts were longer.

With this preparation, students dove into the novel. Olufemi engaged them in a wide variety of activities as they were reading, but the resiliency table and the planning sheet were never far away. Students wrote and talked about their

Figure 7.3   A Brief Bio of Lil Wayne

Lil Wayne's name at birth was Dwayne Michael Carter. His parents are Dwayne Turner and Jacinda Carter. She was 19 when Lil Wayne was born.

Lil Wayne grew up in the Hollygrove section of New Orleans, a very tough and dangerous neighborhood. Shortly after his birth, he and his mother were abandoned by his father. Fortunately, his mother soon married Reginald "Rabbit" McDonald, who became Dwayne's stepfather. Dwayne was in the gifted program at Lafayette Elementary School and was in the drama club in middle school.

Dwayne began to rap at age 12. He developed a reputation as a talented rapper very quickly and wanted to pursue it as a career. He called the rap label Cash Money Records every day and left samples of his freestyle on their answering machine. They signed him on as the label's youngest rapper. He became so dedicated to his rap music that he ended up dropping out of school at age 14.

When he was 12 years old, Lil Wayne became a part of the Williams Brother's band. His mother was afraid that the band would be a bad influence on him, so she pulled him out of Cash Money Records. Lil Wayne responded by running away for a week. After Lil Wayne had convinced his mom that running away was his idea and not the bands', she allowed him to stay with the label.

Lil Wayne faced a number of problems when he was younger. One day when he was playing with a loaded gun, he accidentally pulled the trigger and shot himself. He ended up almost bleeding to death as a result and had to be put on life support for two weeks. When the police came, they verified that the gun was unregistered and that it belonged to his stepdad, who was then sent to jail for half a year. Shortly after Wayne's stepfather was released from prison, he was abducted and murdered.

Lil Wayne has also faced his share of trouble as an adult. On July 22, 2007, Lil Wayne was arrested in New York City following a performance at the Beacon Theatre; the New York City Police Department discovered Lil Wayne and another man smoking marijuana near a tour bus. After taking Lil Wayne into custody, police discovered a .40 caliber pistol on his person. The gun, which was registered to his manager, was in a bag located near the rapper. He was charged with criminal possession of a weapon and marijuana possession. On January 23,

Figure 7.3   A Brief Bio of Lil Wayne *(continued)*

2008, Lil Wayne was arrested alongside two others. His tour bus was stopped by Border Patrol agents near Yuma, Arizona. Police recovered 105 grams (3.7 oz) of marijuana, almost 29 grams (1.0 oz) of cocaine, 41 grams (1.4 oz) of MDMA, and $22,000 in cash. Lil Wayne was charged with four felonies: possession of narcotic drugs for sale, possession of dangerous drugs, misconduct involving weapons, and possession of drug paraphernalia. He was granted permission to travel outside of the state and remain out of custody on the $10,185 bond he posted. On May 6, 2008, Wayne returned to court in Arizona to plead not guilty to the charges. A bench warrant was issued on March 17, 2010 when Lil Wayne did not show up for a final trial management conference. However, the rapper was already in prison, serving a yearlong sentence in Rikers Island on his New York weapons charge. On June 22, 2010 Wayne pled guilty to the Arizona charges. As part of the plea deal he had to serve 36 months of probation.

Lil Wayne was released from Rikers Island for good behavior on November 4, 2010. While he was in prison, Lil Wayne's friends created a website called *Weezy Thanx You*, which published letters written by Lil Wayne in prison. In the first letter, titled "Gone 'til November," the rapper described his daily routine, saying he works out a lot, and reads the Bible every day. He recently tried to put his prison time in perspective, telling *Rolling Stone*: "I look at things as 'Everything is meant to be.' I know it's an experience that I need to have if God's putting me through it."

At the time of his release, Mack Main, the president of Young Money told MTV News that there will be a big homecoming party on Sunday at a Miami strip club in his honor. According to Mack, Lil Wayne's family wants to "just treat him like a king, like the royalty that he is, and make him feel like we really missed him and welcome him back to the family, basically."

Figure 7.4 Planning Sheet

Claim: Lil Wayne will/will not turn his life around

Evidence (from the reading) "What makes you say so?"	Explanation (from the chart) "So what?"	Defense (from your life) "How do you know this is true?"

Figure 7.5 Resilience Simulated Texts

Story 1

Mikey, a fifteen-year-old, did very well in school when he tried. At his old school kids looked up to him for his success, but when he went to a new school things changed. He started hanging out with a new group of boys from his neighborhood. These boys weren't serious about school at all. They were into cutting class, smoking weed, and some of them even sold drugs. As the school year went on, Mikey started to hang out with these kids more and more. His grades dropped and he started to get suspended and in trouble. Mikey's father always brought him back to school but he never really disciplined Mikey. Most of Mikey's teachers gave up on him. They had the attitude that he was headed for failure. But his history teacher didn't give up. He always pushed Mikey to do his best. He was also the track coach, and he was after Mikey to join the team. No matter how many times Mikey said no, his teacher wouldn't take no for an answer.

Question to consider: Will Mikey gain resilience and turn his life around?

Story 2

Chris just got out of placement. He was 16. He was placed for cutting school, suspensions, and for being caught with marijuana. Chris's mother tried her hardest but it was difficult working and raising two children. Chris's brother Jawaan had just come home for good. Jawaan was away in college getting his master's degree in child psychology. While Jawaan was away at school, he still tried to stay in touch with Chris every day but it was very difficult because Jawaan worked full time and took classes full time so the conversations between the two were often short. Also, Chris was often out of the house, so when Jawaan called Chris was not home, and by the time Chris came inside Jawaan was often already sleeping. Chris and Jawaan's father Trey was also coming home soon. He had done a 5–10 year prison stay for being involved in a bank robbery. While Trey was in prison, he got involved with men who showed him how powerful the Black male can be to both his family and community. By the time Trey was ready to leave jail, he had become a different man—a good man who wanted to make sure his family was stable and on the right track.

Question to consider: Will Chris gain resilience and turn his life around?

Story 3

Chrissy was gorgeous. All the guys from the neighborhood wanted to go out with her. She was doing well in school, but then something terrible happened. Chrissy was in the middle of the college application process when her father passed away. Her father was her everything. She felt so empty without him. She started to drink and even use pills. The pain was so much and the drugs were her escape. Chrissy had an older sister Samantha who had just come home from college because she had graduated and had found a job back home. Samantha was also hurt by the passing of their father, but she believed that their father was in heaven so the pain was not so intense. Samantha noticed Chrissy's situation worsening and decided to invite her to church. At church Chrissy met other women who had also made mistakes in their past but now were on the right track. Chrissy knew that the girls at the church were genuine and decided that she would continue to go to the church. But it was hard because the kids in the neighborhood made fun of her for going.

Question to consider: Will Chrissy gain resilience and turn her life around?

Story 4

Crystal had been a great daughter and excellent student in school until she was raped last year by a friend of her mother's. She was 14 when it happened. After the incident Crystal went downhill very fast. Even though she never became disrespectful to her mother, she began to run away from home—sometimes for weeks at a time. She would say to herself, "Why go home. It's not like it's safe there." While Crystal's mother was a successful and educated woman, she could not reach Crystal. It's almost like Crystal had put up a wall. She was angry at her mother who used to be her best friend. Because Crystal and her mother were not getting along too well, she moved in with her grandmother who was more lenient. Her grandmother did care for Crystal but did not have the strength to discipline her. And her grandmother lived in a much worse neighborhood, a place where every night you could see people selling drugs or selling themselves. Crystal, who once was an honor roll student at a high achieving charter school, transferred to a neighborhood high school after the incident and started running with girls who didn't take school seriously. Whenever Crystal's friends were in school, Crystal would be completely off track—walking the hallways instead of going to class. As a result of Crystals sporadic attendance and chronic hall walking, she failed 9th grade. A male teacher who knew Crystal and taught at her school really recognized her potential. He connected Crystal with one of his female best friends, a lawyer who was interested in mentoring a young woman from her old neighborhood.

Question to consider: Will Crystal gain resilience and turn her life around?

predictions about what would happen to the main characters of the novel, drawing on the evidence they had been tracking throughout their reading. The note-taking they were doing on their planning sheets engaged them in composing to plan.

Let's do some more stock-taking and look back at the CCSS. It seems to us that by putting the novel and research on resilience into meaningful conversation, Olufemi was helping his students achieve both writing anchor standards 1 and 9.

However, Olufemi's students were ninth graders and this was the first time they had experienced an inquiry-based curriculum, so there are things Olufemi could have done with a different group of students. Let's think about a few possibilities. After the work on Lil Wayne, one could ask students to research the lives of other celebrities. Different groups of students could be assigned different celebrities and each group could be charged with developing a bio for the class to consider. Writing a celebrity bio is a great occasion to work with students on writing anchor standard 8: "Gather relevant evidence from multiple digital and print sources, assess the credibility and accuracy of each source, and integrate the information while avoiding plagiarism" because so very much of what is written about celebrities seems questionable. Instead of providing the chart to the class, one could ask students to work in groups to do research to compile one themselves, thereby working on at least part of standard 7: "Conduct short as well as more sustained research projects based on focused questions, demonstrating understanding of the subject under investigation." Engaging students in lots of short research experiences such as this one provides excellent preparation for the one or two more sustained research projects that typically comprise the extent of students' research experiences. In addition to having students do a series of informal pieces of writing, he could have had them write a formal essay. Doing so would require them to work on both writing anchor standards 4 and 5: "Produce clear and coherent writing in which the development, organization, and style are appropriate to task, purpose, and audience and the work they did revising their drafts worked to achieving" and "Develop and strengthen writing as needed by planning, revising, editing, rewriting, or trying a new approach."

He could also have asked students to transfer their understanding of resilience into the public policy arena by having them design a program to increase the resilience of adolescents (e.g., a program to avoid substance abuse) or debate the effectiveness of an existing program. If the class has some kind of electronic

➤ *Writing anchor standards 1 and 9*

➤ *Lesson idea*

➤ *Writing anchor standards 4, 5, 7, and 8*

➤ *Lesson idea*

bulletin board such as a wiki, students could work on achieving writing anchor standard 6: "Use technology, including the Internet, to produce and publish writing and to interact and collaborate with others."

➤ *Writing anchor standard 6*

Of course, as much as we admire the teaching Olufemi did, it's only an example. Other possibilities for doing similar work abound. Here's an outline of the process we just discussed:

- Select an inquiry question in which character is central.

- Engage students in considering that question with examples that are close to their experience.

- Engage students in applying research from another discipline or disciplines to shed light on the question both through simulated and through more extended texts.

- Provide multiple opportunities for students to stake their claim on the question through various types of composing.

- Engage students in polishing at least some of their products.

If you do, you'll be helping your students meet the CCSS.

You know that we think the CCSS are important, but the kind of teaching Olufemi did is admirable for an even more important reason. Student after student told Olufemi that what they were talking about in class was helping them think about their lives as well. James, a student who had been a constant attendance and behavioral problem, one day said to Olufemi, "You know what Fadeyibi, I want to be more, what that word again . . . resilient. That's one of my goals." Olufemi was delighted with his students' engagement in and improvement on their reading and writing, but he was even more pleased that they saw their classwork as being useful for the tough lives they were leading.

Another kind of argument that has a similar capacity to foster both personal and intellectual growth is to ask students to think hard about the moral choices that characters make, to consider the alternative choices that were available, and to compose arguments to explain whether and why students agree or disagree with those choices. Many essential questions focus on choice, for example, "How should people respond in the face of oppression?" or "To what do I owe my primary allegiance?" or "To what extent am I responsible for others?" so you'll have plenty of opportunities to focus on this kind of moral argument.

Sometimes an author's position on a character's action is ambiguous. *Sophie's Choice* is a classic example. But even when an author's position on the morality of an action is clear, that doesn't mean it's not arguable. As we noted earlier, it's clear to us that Steinbeck endorses George's decision to kill Lennie, but we're not certain we agree. With a Google search, you can find and read varying responses online from adolescents debating this question.

This kind of moral argument is typically of one of two sorts. Students could argue from consequences similar to something like the following: "Character A made choice B that resulted in consequence C. Had character A made choice D it would have resulted in consequence E. E is preferable to C." That is, for example, "George decided to shoot Lennie in the head which obviously resulted in Lennie's immediate death. Had George decided to run away with Lennie, Lennie would have had a chance to survive. Even a slight chance for survival is better than death." Or students could argue from motive: "Character A made choice B for reason C. C is not an appropriate basis upon which to decide what to do. Had Character A thought about reason D, Character A would have made choice E instead." That is, for example, "George killed Lennie because he was tired of having to watch out for him. So his motive was selfishness. We're supposed to treat others as we want to be treated. Had George applied the Golden Rule, he would have tried to run away with Lenny."

Both types of arguments are complex, much more so than the précis we provide above, as many of the terms are subarguments. That is, the consequence of George's running away is a claim that would have to be established before it can serve as a warrant as would the motive for George's decision to shoot Lennie. But their complexity is just the reason our students need practice at making them. David Brooks (2011) bemoans "how bad [18- to 23-year-olds] are at thinking and talking about moral issues." Maybe that's because we never give them any practice.

➤ Lesson idea

One way to provide the kind of composing to practice students need is to regularly ask them to engage in a kind of moral argumentation. A great way to do so is through good angel/bad angel dramas. A good angel/bad angel drama involves having students act out the kind of conversations you'd see in cartoons when a character faces a decision and a good angel stands on one shoulder trying to persuade the character to make the moral choice and a bad angel stands on the other encouraging a less moral choice. Students could do so either simultaneously in groups of three or the class could collaborate on a single drama with a series of good angels alternating with a series of bad angels as a single character sits in front of the class.

This dramatic activity is useful in preparing students to make arguments. But it's also useful in having them transfer the stuff of their reading to their lives. They face moral choices every day, and we worry that too often they rush into them. They encounter both good angels and bad angels every day. If we can work on the CCSS and help our students make better decisions, too, well, that's something to strive for.

Writing Arguments About Ideas

Throughout this book we've been arguing for embedding the teaching of argument in inquiry units built around essential questions. One important reason to do so is that such units necessitate a focus on thematic generalizations, the ideas an author is grappling with in a text. As we've argued, there's a profound pleasure in living through characters' experience. So too is there a profound pleasure in articulating and examining the ideas that animate a text, saying "Yes, that's the way it is" or "That's a powerful idea to consider" or "I profoundly disagree with that idea."

We've discussed our ideas on theme at length elsewhere (Smith and Wilhelm 2010), but we think it's worth examining a few of our foundational principles as we think about how to prepare students to write arguments about the central ideas of a text. One is that we see theme as a turn in an ongoing cultural conversation. That is, if an author writes a story suggesting, say, that an individual's primary allegiance should be to himself or herself, he or she is putting that story in conversation with texts of others who have suggested that one's primary allegiance is owed to one's country or family or race or religion. Kenneth Burke's (1973) famous parlor metaphor captures our thinking in a nutshell:

> Imagine you enter a parlor. You come late. When you arrive,
> others have long preceded you, and they are engaged in a
> heated discussion, a discussion too heated for them to pause
> and tell you exactly what it is about. In fact, the discussion
> had already begun long before any of them got there, so that
> no one present is qualified to retrace for you all the steps

that had gone before. You listen for a while, until you decide that you have caught the tenor of the argument; then you put in your oar. Someone answers; you answer him; another comes to your defense; another aligns himself against you, to either the embarrassment or gratification of your opponent, depending upon the quality of your ally's assistance. However, the discussion is interminable. The hour grows late, you must depart. And you do depart, with the discussion still vigorously in progress. (110)

Writing an argument about the idea of a text has two steps. The first is to write an interpretive argument as to what the central idea or ideas of a text are. The second is to evaluate those ideas. We've already discussed our ideas on how to help students craft interpretive arguments about a single text. They center on helping students understand the implications of what an author has chosen to do by thinking about what an author could have done. The following activity, one that Michael developed for the *Edge* literature anthology series for struggling and ELL readers, shows how that approach can be specifically directed to work on theme (Figure 7.6). You could use it if you were doing a unit on what makes, sustains, and interferes with friendships.

➤ *Lesson idea*

After students have read the story, they can work together in groups of two or three to discuss the authorial advice suggested in the two different endings before sharing their ideas with the whole class.

The ensuing discussion will focus on paying attention to the details of a text and recognizing the implications of those details when they are understood against imaginable alternatives.

➤ *Lesson idea*

Or if you were doing a unit on what makes, sustains, and interferes with romantic relationships (see Smith and Wilhelm 2010), you could use Frank Stockton's famous "The Lady or the Tiger?" in much the same way. The story is set in a kingdom in which men accused of crimes have to choose one of two doors. Behind one is a lovely maiden. Behind the other is a savage tiger. In the story, the king's daughter takes a lover who is not of her class. The outraged king imprisons the young man. The princess is able to discover which door leads to the lady and which to the tiger. So she's faced with the choice of seeing her lover go to another woman or seeing him be devoured by the tiger. The story closes with

Figure 7.6 Thinking About Themes

Final Cut

Rachel had to admit it; she was looking forward to doing the final project for English. After all, they could choose to work on any of the books they had read and it would be fun to do some kind of artistic response instead of writing another essay. Mr. Hill, Rachel's teacher, was explaining that he wanted them to work in pairs on the project. That made it even better, thought Rachel. She was sure that they'd get a lot of class time to work on the project, so she'd get lots of time to talk with one of her many friends in the class. But Rachel's feelings changed soon after Mr. Hill finished giving the assignment. Just as Rachel was about to go over to her group of friends, Mr. Hill came up to her and said, "Rachel, I want you to work with Jane on this."

Jane! Rachel looked over at her. She had mousy brown hair and wore highwaters and never said anything. Rachel heard one of her friends laugh. This project is ruined, thought Rachel. Jane!

Jane walked over to Rachel's desk and just stood there. Rachel stared straight ahead and didn't say a word until Rachel was fed up. "Oh, sit down," she finally said. Jane slumped into the chair next to Rachel and still didn't say anything. Rachel couldn't stand it anymore. "Okay," she sighed. "You have any ideas about what we should do?"

It turned out that Jane did. "I thought maybe we could do a film," Jane said. Yeah, right, thought Rachel, "How are we going to do that?" Jane went on. "I've been kind of playing around with making films for a while. I could show you." They agreed to meet at the library after school.

After school Rachel and her friends gathered around the library talking and laughing. Rachel didn't even notice when Jane got there, lugging a heavy metal box. One of her friends made things worse by saying, "Rachel, your new friend is here," and laughing loudly. Rachel's face burned.

But once they were settled in the library, things changed. Jane started by taking out a laptop and cuing up a film. "This one's about dreams." It was amazing. Rachel couldn't believe that someone her age had made it. The images and effects were as good as any she'd seen on TV. "And this one's about my dad." Rachel had to choke back the tears watching the short film that was a goodbye to Jane's father who had died suddenly early in the school year. Rachel looked at Jane and said simply, "Can you teach me how to do this?" Jane's answer was equally simple: "Yeah, I can."

After that day Rachel was spending all of her free time with Jane. She learned about the camera. She learned about the editing program. She learned about special effects. She learned what a knowledgeable and patient teacher Jane was. And she learned about her friends. They started getting mad that she wasn't hanging around them so much any more. Every time they saw Jane, one of them was sure to say, "Nice outfit" and laugh.

Figure 7.6   Thinking About Themes *(continued)*

Rachel didn't notice Jane's outfits any more, at least not too much. But she did notice Jane's amazing skill with the camera and her quirky sense of humor. The weeks were flying by.

It was project day. Jane let Rachel set things up to show their film. They'd spent hours and hours on it, but it was worth it. When it was done no one said a word. Then Mr. Hill started to clap. Everyone else joined in, though Rachel noticed her friends weren't clapping quite as much or quite as hard. Rachel looked over at Jane who was blushing and whispered, "Thanks."

After class, Rachel's friends gathered at the door. One said, "So now that that's over, you can get back to normal and drop that geek." Jane was back in the room, packing up equipment. Rachel looked hard at the girls and turned without saying a word. She walked back into the class and started to help with the equipment. Jane flashed her a little smile. Rachel smiled back. "Want to get a cup of coffee after school?"

Imagine that the author of the story is an advice columnist. Pretend that you are the author and write a letter that responds to the following request for advice:

Dear High School Hotline,

I have no friends at school. Everyday it's the same thing. Kids make fun of my clothes, my hair, and even my music. Most of the time I don't care. I love my music. I have a deal worked out with the music teacher that I can practice piano during lunch. He's after me to join the jazz band, but I'm not going to do it. The idea of spending more time at school just makes me sick. I do 4 or 5 hours of practice every day after school and when I do it, I'm as happy as can be. Then the next day comes and I have to go back to school. I hate it. What should I do?

Sour Note in Sausalito

Now pretend the story ended this way:

After class, Rachel's friends gathered at the door. One said, "So now that that's over, you can get back to normal and drop that geek." Jane was back in the room, packing up equipment. Rachel smiled at the girls and returned to the classroom. She started to help with the equipment. Jane flashed her a little smile. Rachel smiled back. "After school maybe you and I and the others," she nodded her head in the direction of the door where the other girls were gathered, "could go to the mall. We could maybe get you some new clothes." Jane responded quickly, "That's just what I was hoping you'd say. I can't wait."

What would the author of a story with this new ending say to Sour Note in Sausalito? Talk with your partner(s) about whether and how the advice of the author of this new story would be different.

her signaling the young man which door to choose. Stockton doesn't reveal the choice and instead asks readers to "engage in a study of the human heart" and determine for themselves which choice the princess made.

It's fun to talk about which choice the princess made. But we think it's more profitable to ask students to imagine that the princess' choice was the lady and then pretend they were the author of the story that ended that way. Then we'd ask them to identify which of the quotes in Figure 7.7 they would most agree with and those with which they would most disagree.

➤ *Lesson idea*

This activity helps students understand right from the beginning of a unit the nature of the ongoing conversation in which the texts you are reading is embedded. Of course, you don't have to find a catalog of quotes to do so. You could write out competing understandings yourself in what George Hillocks (cf., 2011) calls an *opinionnaire.* Say, for example, that you were doing a unit on the question "What makes me, me?" You could begin with an opinionnaire like Figure 7.8.

➤ *Lesson idea*

The ensuing discussion should focus on the items that are most clearly in dispute. Once again, drawing on the Toulmin questions ("What makes you say so?" and "So what?") will help students elucidate their understandings.

Once you've compiled a series of quotes or written a series of statements yourself, you should return to them again and again. We suggest collecting and saving the opinionnaires students fill out at the beginning of a unit. As the unit goes on, you can ask students to fill out the same opinionnaire from the perspective of each of the authors in the unit. Then you can ask them to write an argument explaining why they think an author is right or wrong. Authorizing their ideas right from the start through the opinionnaire and establishing that the ideas about which they're thinking are highly contested ones will make it far more likely that students will feel confident enough to argue with an author.

The evidence for such an argument would have to be explaining situations that are in conflict with the thematic generalization(s) an author wishes readers to infer from his or her text, drawn from students' lives, their knowledge of the world, or their reading of other texts. The challenge for students will be to write accurate summaries of those situations. We make suggestions for helping students write summaries in our book on informative writing (Wilhelm, Smith, and Fredricksen 2012), so we won't focus on our ideas here. But we do want to stress our strong belief that writing an accurate summary is a difficult task indeed, one that takes plenty of practice. The good news is that warranting such

Figure 7.7   Thoughts of Love

1. **ANNE MORROW LINDBERGH:**

   Him that I love, I wish to be free—even from me.

2. **C. S. LEWIS:**

   Why love if losing hurts so much? We love to know that we are not alone.

3. **EURIPIDES:**

   He is not a lover who does not love forever.

4. **MARGARET ANDERSON:**

   In real love you want the other person's good. In romantic love you want the other person.

5. **ROSE WALKER:**

   Have you even been in love? Horrible, isn't it? It makes you so vulnerable. It opens your chest and it opens your heart and it means someone can get inside you and mess you up. You build up all these defenses. You build up this whole armor, for years, so nothing can hurt you, then one stupid person, no different from any other stupid person, wanders into your stupid life. . . .

6. **ST. AUGUSTINE:**

   Better to have loved and lost, than to have never loved at all.

Figure 7.8 Opinionnaire

Please indicate whether you strongly agree (SA), agree (A), disagree (D), or strongly disagree (SD) with each of the following statements:

All people become who they are by what they do in their lives.

    SA   **A**   **D**   **SD**

No matter how hard you try, you can't escape the influence of where and when you live.

    SA   **A**   **D**   **SD**

People are all the same. They just differ by how much money they have.

    SA   **A**   **D**   **SD**

Men are men and women are women. That's just the way things are.

    SA   **A**   **D**   **SD**

Our families make us who we are.

    SA   **A**   **D**   **SD**

You're nothing more than what your genes say you are.

    SA   **A**   **D**   **SD**

arguments is relatively easy, as the warrants are likely to be something like "The incidence of such exceptions to an author's generalization call its usefulness into question."

➤ *Writing anchor standard 8*

The kind of writing and instruction we're calling for here seems to us to be consistent with writing anchor standard 8: "Gather relevant information from multiple print and digital sources, assess the credibility and accuracy of each source, and integrate the information while avoiding plagiarism." In fact, we'd argue that the instruction and assignments we advocate here go beyond the standards. Assessing the veracity or utility of the kind of abstract generalization that a literary text gets after seems to us to be much more challenging than simply assessing a source's factual accuracy or making a judgment about its credibility.

Evaluative Arguments

Another kind of literary argument that students could write is evaluative arguments. Our students offered plenty of unsolicited evaluative arguments, usually of the "This sucks" variety. We're aware of the maxim *"De gustibus non est disputandum"* (There's no disputing matters of taste), but all of us violate that maxim from time to time. In fact, disputes over matters of taste abound in our culture. Look at the Rotten Tomatoes website or read the comments after a YouTube video and you'll see. But what is lacking, we're afraid, is thoughtfully developed evaluative arguments.

Evaluative arguments always hinge on warrants. They proceed something like this:

Text A can be characterized by _____.

_____ is/is not a feature of high-quality texts.

I know this because _____.

Of course, there's more to it than simply filling in the blanks. Much like arguments about the idea of a text, making an evaluative argument requires subarguments. Just as one cannot simply assert what the theme of a text is, so too can one not simply assert that it is realistic or unrealistic, broadly appealing or narrowly appealing, fast-paced or slow-moving, and so on.

But even when the features of a text have been established, one has to work to answer the "So what?" question. And as we've argued again and again, the key to helping students do that kind of work is to provide plenty of practice.

One good place to start is to have students examine the evaluative arguments of others. A great way to do so is to have students look at the evaluative arguments made by celebrity judges on one of the ubiquitous competition shows. For example, in the show *Chopped*, a panel of celebrity chefs judges the cooking of four lesser-known chefs, who have to prepare an appetizer, entrée, and dessert using ingredients determined by the show. After each course, the chef whose food is found least satisfactory is "chopped," until a single chef emerges victorious. Students could analyze the show to see when data were accepted and when they had to be established. They could see different warrants being discussed as one judge emphasizes creativity and another taste. Of course, any similar show could serve as well.

> ➤ *Lesson idea*

The next step would be to have students make their own judgments. One way to do so is to ask students to rank the effectiveness of similar texts that have similar purposes. For example, you could ask students to work in groups to rank the effectiveness of four or five car, clothing, or perfume ads. It's important that the products advertised and the intended audiences are very similar. You want students to base their rankings on what they see as the effectiveness of the ads and not whether they prefer, say, an SUV over a sedan. Or you could have them rank four to five editorials or editorial cartoons critiquing President Obama or the Republican congressional leadership. Or you could have them act as judges for one of the many talent shows currently on TV. The possibilities are limitless. The group work will only be effective if students come up with different rankings. If they do, the ensuing discussion will require them both to establish a safe starting point ("This ad is cooler" simply won't carry the day) and to articulate a warrant ("So what if the ad features a well-known celebrity?").

But those warrants likely would simply be asserted. As a next step we recommend having students debate the relative merits of two currently popular romantic comedies, video games, sit-coms, or cartoons and having students do Internet research on the qualities on which people make evaluative judgments. In a few minutes of surfing the web, we found the following warrants in discussions of what makes a good video game:

- "They let you gain new abilities or weapons that you *need* in order to progress."

- "In various Internet forums and game-magazine columns about video and board games, a good plot or storyline is cited as essential to a good game."

- "Gameplay is the coup de grace, and I will explain why. When you play a video game, and you start it off, you try out all of the buttons, and what the main character can do. That's all gravy, but you want to see what other characters can do. Communication with Non Player Characters or NPCs is gameplay."

- "First things first, a good video game needs to have rules and controls that can be easily understood."

In order to determine which (if any) of these warrants students would employ, they would have to do just what they are called upon to do in writing anchor standard 8: "Gather relevant evidence from multiple digital and print sources, assess the credibility and accuracy of each source and integrate the information while avoiding plagiarism."

➤ *Writing anchor standard 8*

As a transition to writing evaluative arguments about literary texts, students could examine reviews on Amazon.com and analyze whether the disagreements about a text are a function of the data presented or the warrants employed. More than 3,120 readers wrote evaluations of *The Catcher in the Rye*, for example, and 534 gave it one or two stars. Engaging the whole class in rewriting a review or two to make them more effective is an efficient way to provide practice. Another possibility would be to have students practice on less complex texts like children's books. You could start the ball rolling by sharing an evaluation of a popular book. Michael, for example, modeled an evaluation by arguing that Shel Silverstein's *The Giving Tree* was a bad book because it depicted a woman's willingness to sacrifice herself for an unworthy man and good children's books ought to provide positive role models. Plenty of talk ensued about both the data and the claim.

After this preparation, students will be ready to write more formal evaluative arguments about the texts they are reading in class. Of course, if they are to be genuinely engaged in doing so, it's crucial that the evaluative question be an authentic one. Michael remembers being asked by a humanities teacher to explain why the music of *West Side Story* was superior to the music of other popular musicals. If we want students to seriously engage with evaluative questions, we can't simply assert the superiority of our evaluations. Once students have completed their reviews we suggest having them post them, a great way to raise the stakes of the games while at the same time working to achieve writing anchor standard 6: "Use technology, including the Internet, to produce and publish writing and to interact and collaborate with others."

➤ *Writing anchor standard 6*

The evaluative arguments we've been talking about thus far have been aesthetic evaluations. As educators, however, we are more commonly engaged in instructional evaluations. As teaching professionals we have to evaluate whether we should teach a text or not. Our professional lives abound with controversies about those evaluations. Should we teach *Huckleberry Finn*? Jeff thinks the book at its heart is moral and provides the occasion for teaching a whole host of interpretive strategies, so he votes yes. Jim would also vote yes, though he'd warrant his argument by saying that it provides an opportunity to begin or extend a conversation about the history of race relations in America. Michael's not so sure. He thinks that the book is racist, not because of the use of the word *nigger* but rather because Twain seems to count on readers' dismissing Tom's treatment of Jim in the section on Jim's escape. If he were to teach it, it would only be because the novel affords a chance to seriously discuss the nature of racism.

Other possibilities for engaging students in educational debates abound. Larry Johannessen, Betsy Kahn, and Carolyn Calhoun Walter (2009) suggest the following as a possible assignment for *To Kill a Mockingbird*:

➤ *Lesson idea*

> Some readers have criticized Harper Lee's *To Kill a Mockingbird*
> for not presenting good female role models. They argue that
> the novel has strong male role models, including Atticus Finch,
> Tom Robinson, Jem, and Sheriff Tate, but that it is lacking in
> good female role models. Others argue that there are good
> female role models among the female characters, like Miss
> Maudie, Calpurnia, Aunt Alexandra, Mrs. Dubose, and even
> Scout. Does *To Kill a Mockingbird* lack good female role models?

They propose engaging students in discussing whether the focal character of cases such as the following is a good role model to give students practice in articulating warrants, that is, general rules of what makes a good role model:

Lucy Lee had a tough life. She dropped out of school at age 15 when she had her first child. At age 17, she was a single mother with three children and no support from the father. She received welfare in order to survive. At age 20, with the help of her mother who watched her children, she was able to go back to school at night. She received her GED and was accepted at a local college. At 26, she graduated with a college degree in accounting and was able to get a good job that enables her to have her own house and provide for her children.

But that's just one possible area of argument for that book. A couple of years ago subscribers to one of the listservs to which Michael belongs had an extended exchange about *To Kill a Mockingbird*, motivated by the posting of an essay by Malcolm Gladwell (2009) that critiques the book. The extended exchange raised a number of interesting issues about the merits of the book: To what extent does Lee's apparent endorsement of incrementalism undermine its value in the classroom? How about its portrayal of the Klan? Or its portrayal of African American characters?

Much like the other evaluative argument, evaluations of whether to teach a book depend on warrants—the criteria one ought to use in deciding what to teach. It's important, therefore, to give students practice in articulating those criteria. Figure 7.9 will be useful in helping students do just that.

When we talked about writing arguments about ideas, we detailed how doing so prepared students to meet many of the CCSS anchor standards. The evaluative arguments of the sort we describe seem to us to have all the same benefits. They also provide an excellent opportunity for students to become researchers themselves. If the question is, say, "Should *Huck Finn* be taught?" students could interview other students who have read the book and could use their experience as data. Or they could interview teachers, parents, and other students about just what it is that makes a book worth teaching as a way to research warrants they could employ in making their determinations.

> *Writing anchor standards 7–9*

This kind of research provides another opportunity to exceed the CCSS. Writing anchor standards 7–9 all focus on research, but all seem to us to imply that that research will be with secondary textual sources. Some research in education is text-based, but much more of it requires the kind of data collection

Figure 7.9   Should We Teach It?

Below are seven short descriptions of different books. On the basis of those descriptions, rank the books from the one that you feel should most definitely be taught to your class (1) to the one you feel most strongly about not teaching (7).

Book 1: Provides a wonderfully accurate and heartbreaking portrayal of the day to day life of a working class family in the Philippines. It's short and will be easy to read for most adolescents.

Rank _____

Book 2: Provides an absolutely frightening description of what can happen as a consequence of teen alcohol and drug use. Warning: It's not for the squeamish. The book features many sexual situations and lots of rough language.

Rank _____

Book 3: A modern classic that demonstrates how the beauty of language can transport readers into an entirely new world. Who would have thought that the London of 1850 would be such a wonderful place to visit? The kind of book that makes readers slow down as they near the end so they won't have to put it down.

Rank _____

Book 4: A laugh riot. The story of five young friends trying to make it in New York after they graduate from a prestigious Ivy League college. The story may not be realistic, but it is hilarious.

Rank _____

Book 5: More and more colleges are requiring this book and it's easy to see why. It makes a powerful argument about why college matters and tells a dramatic story of how one American young man overcame adversity and successfully completed school.

Rank _____

Book 6: A teen bestseller that proves that young people's fascination with fantasy doesn't end with *Harry Potter*. The book doesn't have Rowlings' memorable characters but it does have action, action, and more action.

Rank _____

Book 7: A classic that has been taught for generations. A challenge for many students because of its complex language and adult themes, but one that is sure to pay off, both in getting students ready for college and in encouraging hard thinking about universal themes.

Rank _____

© 2012 by Michael W. Smith, Jeffrey D. Wilhelm, and James E. Fredricksen, from *Oh, Yeah?!* Portsmouth, NH: Heinemann.

we described above. It seems to us that we are doing more to prepare students for college if we provide both the opportunity for and instruction in the kind of research that members of our discipline actually do.

Before we close, we want to be clear that the four kinds of arguments we discuss here are not exhaustive. Plenty of other opportunities exist. You could engage students in analyzing their own and their classmates' think-alouds to make an argument about the extent to which disagreements about interpretations are rooted in the texts and which are rooted in the readers. After doing work to help them understand various theoretical perspectives (see Deborah Appleman's outstanding *Critical Encounters* [2009] for a comprehensive description of engaging ways to do just that), you could have them write an argument evaluating the relative merits of one perspective as compared with others. We hope that this chapter has occasioned your thinking about many more.

We also want to stress that you'll have to choose which kind (or kinds) of literary arguments you'll include in your units. Our suggestion is to have students write at least one literary and at least one nonliterary argument in each unit and to make sure that those arguments are related in some way. You can see how this plays out in the sample unit that's included in the appendix.

Finally, we want to stress that we know that our English language arts classrooms too often do not feature the kinds of rich argumentative exchanges we endorse here. Instead we tend to try to lead students to what we want them to think. It's time to change that state of affairs if we want to help our students meet the CCSS. It's time to change that state of affairs if we want them to experience the intellectual excitement that brought us to the profession in the first place.

CHAPTER 8

Focusing on Form

In Chapters 6 and 7 we focused primarily on developing strategies to generate content; that is, on procedural knowledge of substance. In this chapter, we'll focus primarily on developing strategies for effectively rendering that content, that is, on procedural knowledge of form, the kind of knowledge that writing anchor standard 4 seems to be getting after: "Produce clear and coherent writing in which the development, organization, and style are appropriate to task, purpose, and audience." Again, we want to note that as students learn to generate the structures of argument, they will also learn to name those structures and how they work, thereby developing declarative knowledge of form as well.

➤ *Writing anchor standards 4*

Developing Sentence Sense

Let's start by thinking about the syntactic knowledge students need to produce effective arguments. Consider just a couple examples from the letters to the editor section of the *New York Times* the day this chapter was first drafted (December 20, 2011):

- The National Transportation Safety Board's call for a ban on cell phone use by drivers, including hands-free devices, while no doubt motivated by good intentions and troubling statistics, is nevertheless ill considered.

- The allegation that Bahrain is a "brutal, family-run dictatorship" disregards the fact that in Bahrain, a transitional democracy, not all power is vested in the king.

Of course, not every sentence in every letter is so complex. But these examples reveal just how complicated it can be to develop an argument (and craft its constituent sentences), for inherent in doing so, as we discussed in our explanation of Toulmin's model, is both making your own case and responding to the case of another, whether it has been explicitly made or whether it's anticipated. Articulating the relationships among ideas often requires complex syntax. So too does qualifying a claim. So too does authorizing the source of some piece of information. We could go on, but suffice it to say that writers of arguments have their work to do on the sentence level. And it's not just letter writers to the *New York Times* who have to manage this complexity. Remember our discussion in Chapter 6 of the simulation that Mary Beth Monahan employed in her sixth-grade classroom. Here's a sentence from a paper we quoted: "If we now assume that the crack somehow did get by Kate and it leaked, the bottle would be lighter instead of heavier."

As we argued in *Getting It Right* (Smith and Wilhelm 2007), one way to help students develop the syntactic complexity they need is to use sentence combining. The two most recent comprehensive reviews of writing research (Hillocks 1986a, Graham and Perin 2007) have both made it clear that sentence combining is an effective way to improve students' writing. Graham and Perin provide a succinct description of sentence combining and a statement of its effectiveness:

> Sentence combining involves teaching students to construct more complex and sophisticated sentences through exercises in which two or more basic sentences are combined into a single sentence. Teaching adolescents how to write increasingly complex sentences in this way enhances the quality of their writing.

If you google "sentence combining," you'll see a variety of books that feature sentence combining. You'll notice that sentence combining exercises are of two sorts. In *open-combining* activities, writers combine the simple sentences (also called *kernels*) in whatever way they choose. *Closed-sentence combining* exercises restrict the writer's choices to a specific structure. You should take a look to find the book that's the best match for your students. Or you can develop your own sentence-combining activities. It's not hard. All you need to do is to break down complex sentences into the basic sentences (or kernels) of which they are constructed. You can use your students' papers as the source of these sentences, your own writing, or that of a published author.

One advantage of creating your own sentence-combining exercises is that you can make them relevant to the inquiry the class is pursuing. Here's an example of one little exercise that would be relevant to an inquiry on one of the essential questions we discussed last chapter: "What makes a person resilient?"

➤ *Lesson idea*

Some people think about resilience.

The thinking is about causes.

The causes are important.

The causes are personal attributes.

Other people disagree.

They think about other causes.

They think about social supports.

One social support is the community.

Another social support is the school.

These kernels can be combined in many ways. Here are some possibilities students might come up with (complete with problematic wording and correctness errors):

- Some people think that the primary cause of resilience is someone's personal attributes, but others think that social supports in the school and community are more important.

- People disagree about the primary cause of resilience, some see your personal attributes as most important, and others see community and school supports as most important.

- Disagreements about the primary causes of resilience center on the importance of personal attributes as compared with the social supports the community and school can provide.

- While some people see the primary cause of resilience to be a person's attributes, others believe that social supports from the community and school are more significant.

We suggest having students work on a combination (maybe a Do Now or entrance ticket for the beginning of the class) or set of combinations (we typically have students work on four to five at a time) and then having them share their combinations with the class. After explaining any correctness issues that might emerge (e.g., the comma splice in the second alternative), the class could discuss which combination they liked best and why. Or as an alternative, you could compose multiple combinations and have the students rank them in terms of their effectiveness before asking students to do some combining on their own.

If you want students to work on a particular structure, say an introductory adverbial clause as in the fourth example above, you could require that they all produce one. (As an aside: we would suggest limiting the grammatical terms that you use to the absolute minimum. See Smith and Wilhelm 2007 for a book-length discussion of the teaching of grammar.) You could provide possible subordinating conjunctions or allow students to develop their own. Here are some possibilities students might produce:

- Although some contend that the primary cause of resilience to be a person's attributes, others believe that social supports from the community and school are more significant.

- Whereas some people see the primary cause of resilience to be a person's attributes, others believe that social supports from the community and school are more significant.

- Even though some people think that the primary cause of resilience is a person's attributes, others think that social supports from the community and school are more significant.

We suggest proceeding with the same kind of discussion with closed combinations as we suggested with open ones. You'll be surprised at how nuanced those discussions can become. Which subordinating conjunction works best? Which verb choice? Is using different verbs in each clause more effective than employing the same verb? How about *your* versus *a person's*? And on and on.

➤ *Writing standard 4; language standards; reading standards 3–5*

Having students do the kind of focused writing with extensive follow-up discussions seems to us not only to help students achieve the Core writing anchor standard 4 but also all of the anchor standards for language and Core reading anchor standards 3–5.

➤ *Lesson idea*

Another possible way to help students develop the requisite sentence-level skills is to have them practice using sentence templates. Graff and Birkenstein's (2010) *They Say/I Say: The Moves That Matter in Academic Writing* is a wonderful source for a wide variety of templates. They argue that their aim is to demystify and hence democratize academic discourse and note that their aim is not "to stifle critical thinking but to be direct with students about the key rhetorical moves it comprises" (xxii).

The book was written for college students, but we think it could be modified for use with much younger students as well. To give you a flavor of the book, we'll share the templates they provide for introducing "standard views" (23):

- Americans have always believed that individual effort can triumph over circumstances.

- Conventional wisdom has it that _____.

- Common sense seems to dictate that _____.

- The standard way of thinking about topic X has it that _____.

- It is often said that _____.

- My whole life I have heard that _____.

- You would think that _____.

- Many people assume that _____.

The book provides templates for sharing what others are saying, for responding to what others have said, and for tying it all together.

As we've noted throughout this book, if students are to learn something so deeply they can transfer it to new situations they need lots of practice and plenty of opportunities for reflection. You can provide that practice and those opportunities for reflection by having students engage with material relevant to the inquiry the class is pursuing. We'll spin out a short sequence of activities that could also be used in a unit built around the question "What makes a person resilient?"

Remember that one of the benefits we see in organizing your class around inquiry units built around an essential question is that they provide plenty of opportunities both for students to put literary and nonliterary texts into meaningful conversation and for students to do lots of independent research. When students write arguments that draw on multiple texts, they'll have to effectively employ reporting verbs—those that alert the reader that someone else's words are being quoted or paraphrased. That means not relying only on the old standbys: She writes, "_____" or She says, "_____."

➤ *Writing anchor standards 7–10; reading anchor standards 7–10*

➤ *Writing standards 8, language standards 1–6*

Graff and Birkenstein (2010) provide a comprehensive list of possibilities (39–40). We find the following verbs chart developed by the University of Adelaide (available on its website) even more useful as it provides not only a list of words but also suggests something about the force of those words:

	Weaker position	Neutral position	Stronger position
addition		adds	
advice		advises	
agreement	admits, concedes	accepts, acknowledges, agrees, concurs, confirms, recognizes	applauds, congratulates, extols, praises, supports
argument and persuasion	apologizes	assures, encourages, interprets, justifies, reasons	alerts, argues, boasts, contends, convinces, emphasizes, exhorts, forbids, insists, proves, promises, persuades, threatens, warns
believing	guesses, hopes, imagines	believes, claims, declares, expresses, feels, holds, knows, maintains, professes, subscribes to, thinks	asserts, guarantees, insists, upholds
conclusion		concludes, discovers, finds, infers, realizes	
disagreement and ques-tioning	doubts, questions	challenges, debates, disagrees, questions, requests, wonders	accuses, attacks, complains, contradicts, criticizes, denies, discards, disclaims, discounts, dismisses, disputes, disregards, negates, objects to, opposes, refutes, rejects
discussion	comments	discusses, explores	reasons
emphasis			accentuates, emphasizes, highlights, stresses, underscores, warns
evaluation and examination		analyzes, appraises, assesses, compares, considers, contrasts, critiques, evaluates, examines, investigates, understands	blames, complains, ignores, scrutinizes, warns
explanation		articulates, clarifies, explains	
presentation	confuses	comments, defines, describes, estimates, forgets, identifies, illustrates, implies, informs, instructs, lists, mentions, notes, observes, outlines, points out, presets, remarks, reminds, reports, restates, reveals, shows, states, studies, tells, uses	announces, promises
suggestion	alleges, intimates, speculates	advises, advocates, hypothesizes, posits, postulates, proposes, suggests, theorizes	asserts, recommends, urges

Having declarative knowledge of the possibilities that exist is important, but having procedural knowledge, that is, being able to employ those words, is even more important. And once again, if students are to develop the ability of effectively employing the words of others they'll need plenty of practice.

One way to provide that practice is to have students work with abstracts of articles that relate to the essential question. You can easily find such articles online, particularly through your state's interlibrary online database services. Students can also be asked to find such articles, providing them with valuable experience that helps them to meet CCSS' standards for accessing data as well as writing standards 7–9 and reading standards 7–9.

➤ *Lesson idea*

➤ *Writing standards 7–9, reading standards 7–9*

Here are abstracts of two articles that take up the question "What makes a person resilient?" in one way or another: "Educational Resilience in African American Adolescents" (Cunningham and Swanson 2010) and "Fostering Social-Emotional Resilience Among Latino Youth" (Reyes and Elias 2011):

> The purpose of this article was to examine factors within the school context that facilitates educational resilience among African American high school students. The authors expected academic self-esteem to be positively associated with future expectations (academic and general). They expected perceptions of school-based social support to have positive associations with achievement outcomes. They also investigated if there are gender differences in any of the variables. The participants were 206 African American adolescents (65.54% female) who resided in a large urban city in the south-central geographic area of the United States. Results supported the notion that educational resilience was associated with perceived school support, academic self-esteem, and mother's work history. The results have implications for educators and other professionals who are interested in promoting educational resilience in high school students.
>
> National statistics reveal that Latino youth face significant challenges and engage in many risky behaviors that can hinder positive development and well-being, such as attempted suicide, lifetime cocaine use, unprotected sex, and dropping out of school. However, these statistics obscure the fact that many

Latino youth are developing well despite exposure to significant adversity. A critical question that lies before researchers, educators, and policy makers is how to improve the health, well-being, and achievement of more Latino youth. This article considers conceptual issues related to resilience and culture, risk, and protective factors relevant to Latinos and the role schools play in promoting resilience. Special attention is paid to the building of child-based resources, such as social-emotional competencies, and social system resources, such as a caring school climate.

After reading the abstracts together and clarifying their meanings, you could ask students to write a sentence explaining what position each set of writers has on the contention that personal factors are the most significant predictor of an adolescent's resilience. (Think of the practice students are getting here as readers and as summarizers familiarizing themselves with abstracts and even shorter summaries.) Or you could have students work together to write a sentence or two that articulates some kind of relationship between the two articles. Or if students needed more support, you could start by having them use the chart to complete sentences like the following:

➤ *Reading anchor standards 7, 9*

- Although Swanson and Cunningham _____ that one's mother's work history is associated with academic resilience, they _____ that perceived school support is also crucial.

- Reyes and Elias _____ that building child-based resources is critically important to a student's resilience.

A next step would be to go through the articles themselves and have students select quotes that take a position on the question and to write sentences that introduce the quote using one of the following templates:

- Author 1 and Author 2 (*reporting verb*) that ". . . ."

- Author 1 and Author 2 (*reporting verb*) (*describing word*) that ". . . ."

- As Author 1 and Author 2 (*reporting verb*), ". . . ."

- As Author 1 and Author 2 (*reporting verb*) (*describing word*), ". . . ."

- Author 1 and Author 2 (*reporting verb*) (*phrase summary of quote*): "...."

- Author 1 and Author 2 (*describing word*) (*reporting verb*) (*phrase summary of quote*): "...."

You should present the templates by modeling them, explaining both why you made the choices of reporting verbs and modifiers that you did and why you amended the templates, for example, by switching the position of the modifier. We'll illustrate some possibilities below. Of course, your examples will vary based on the quotes you and your students have selected.

- Swanson and Cunningham emphasize that "...."

- Swanson and Cunningham argue convincingly that "...."

- As Swanson and Cunningham contend, "...."

- As Swanson and Cunningham forcefully declare, "...."

- Swanson and Cunningham investigate a competing view: "...."

- Swanson and Cunningham succinctly articulate their primary argument: "...."

Because conscious control is so important to transfer, it's crucial to have students do the same kind of explaining you did as you modeled when they present their alternative either to the whole-class or in small-group discussions. These activities meet a wide variety of the CCSS standards: reading anchor standards 1–3, and aspects of all the other reading standards; writing anchor standards 1 and 4; speaking and listening anchor standards 1, 3, and 4.

> ➤ *Reading standards 1–3, writing standards 1 and 4, speaking and listening standards 1, 3, and 4*

Of course, your decision about how many and what kind of templates you'll provide will vary depending on your kids and their needs. But what shouldn't vary is your commitment to providing students plenty of practice throughout the unit on developing the syntactic complexity they'll need to write effective arguments.

Thinking About Organization

Of course, knowledge of form requires much more than knowledge of sentences. Whether your students are writing single paragraphs or entire research papers, they'll have to think hard about how they organize the larger pieces of their arguments. The reason they have to think so hard is that there's no one right approach. Consider, for example, how three reviews of the recently released *We Bought a Zoo* begin:

- Benjamin Mee (Matt Damon) can't stop thinking about his late wife. Wherever he goes, he's reminded of her, and he's happy to keep those memories alive. (Calvin Wilson, *St. Louis Post-Dispatch*)

- Genuinely charming, treacle-free family films are tough to find these days, so I'm happy to heartily recommend "We Bought a Zoo" as heartwarming holiday fare that even jaded adults can share with the kids. (Lou Lumenick, *New York Post*)

- Pap, but easygoing pap with a cast you can live with for a couple of hours, "We Bought a Zoo" is co-writer and director Cameron Crowe's adaptation of a memoir by Benjamin Mee entitled "We Bought a Zoo: The Amazing True Story of a Young Family, a Broken Down Zoo, and the 200 Wild Animals That Change Their Lives Forever." (Michael Phillips, *Chicago Tribune*)

Wilson begins his review with a summary that he uses as data. Lumenick begins his with the criterion of judgment he's applying—in other words, the warrant. Only Michael Phillips makes the conventional move of starting with the claim.

Think of public policy arguments. We've mentioned the health care debate earlier and it provides an illustration of the range of organizational possibilities a writer might choose. Writers in favor of health care reform might begin their argument by establishing the warrant, that it's the obligation of government to provide for the welfare and therefore the health security of all of its citizens. Other writers might choose to begin by trying to defuse concerns about single-payer options, by posing and then responding to a reservation. Or still other writers might want to state their claim and then move immediately to the data on how many people are uninsured and what this costs them and society at large.

We understand that formulas are comfortable, a fact borne out by the ubiquity of the five-paragraph essay. However, the CCSS challenge us to prepare our students for college and for work in the world and it's important to understand that five-paragraph essays don't exist in either place. Talk to a college writing teacher and we'll bet he or she will tell you that one of the first orders of business is to unteach the five paragraph essay (Jeff can vouch that this is an annual topic of the Writing Committee at Boise State University). Indeed the *Framework for Success in Post-Secondary Writing* (2011), coauthored by the Council of Writing Program Administrators, the National Council of Teachers of English, and the National Writing Project, argues bluntly that

> Standardized writing curricula or assessment instruments that emphasize formulaic writing for non-authentic audiences will not reinforce the habits of mind and the experiences necessary for success as students encounter the demands of postsecondary education. (3)

And the Educational Testing Service report detailing the design of the PARCC and Smarter Balanced tests (more on these tests next chapter) has a subhead titled "Discarding the Five-Paragraph Straightjacket."

We'll grant that it makes sense to begin with some kind of introduction and to close with some sort of conclusion. But the number and function of body paragraphs will vary depending upon the nature of the argument and the rhetorical situation. The CCSS clearly recognize that fact. Let's look at Core writing anchor standards 4 and 5, the ones that this chapter addresses:

4. Produce clear and coherent writing in which the development, organization, and style are appropriate to task, purpose, and audience.

5. Develop and strengthen writing as needed by planning, revising, editing, rewriting, or trying a new approach.

The notion of appropriateness in writing anchor standard 4 means the CCSS understand that one size doesn't fit all. Development, organization, and style all vary as a function of task, purpose, and audience. (We'd add *rhetorical situation* to the list.) The notion of "trying a new approach" clearly means that the CCSS recognize that more than one approach may be viable.

We've written elsewhere (Smith and Wilhelm 2007, 2010; Wilhelm, Smith, and Fredricksen 2012) about the correspondence concept that's currently popular in cognitive science (cf., Bereiter 2004; Nickerson 1985). The correspondence concept holds that teachers should teach toward actual expert practice. That is, teachers should design instruction to move students progressively toward how expert readers and writers go about their business. If we don't, we are teaching mythology and not reading and writing. We don't want to overstate the case, but we believe that teaching formulaic writing that does not exist beyond secondary schools is actually moving students *away from* expertise. Doing so, we would argue, actually makes students stupider rather than smarter since they are being moved away from real-world expertise.

What real writers have to do when they craft an argument is to think hard about why they do what they do. That's why we suggest that students write annotated arguments in which they identify one or two or three (depending on the students) substantive, stylistic, and organizational moves that they make and explain why they did what they did. If your students type their papers, they can easily provide annotations by using the comment function in their word-processing program. If they don't, sticky notes will do the trick. Then you can comment on their comments, either in conferences or as part of your assessment. This kind of composing to transfer promotes metacognitive awareness and the reflection required on the drafts of the performance tasks of the PARCC and Smarter Balanced tests.

➤ *Lesson idea*

We know that prior to this chapter the instruction that we detailed was primarily directed to generating content. It's crucially important that students make claims that are worth defending and that they support those claims with data and warrants. But it's equally important that students render their arguments effectively, that they write clear and compelling sentences, and that they organize those sentences in such a way that they have the greatest possible impact. We believe that focusing on form as we have suggested here will help them do just that.

A Few Words About Assessment

In-Class Assessments

When we have worked with teachers to include the kind of comprehensive writing instruction that we're calling for in this book, we often hear something like the following: "Okay, I hear what you're saying. I'd like to include more writing in my classroom. I really would. But I just can't spend any more time grading than I already do." We get it. We really do. But here's the thing: we know that by increasing the amount of argument writing your students do you can actually reduce the amount of out-of-school time you spend grading and responding to it.

We know that it seems counterintuitive, but let's explain. In the first place, the extensive and focused instruction that we're calling for helps operationalize shared understandings. Such operationalizing has two benefits. One, it makes communicating with students much easier. For example, once you've done the "Is It Safe?" activity that we explain in Chapter 5, you can glance over a student's shoulder as she is writing and say simply, "Doesn't seem safe to me." The student will understand that you're bringing forward all of the work you've done on data and will know what you mean. And when you're providing written responses to students, you can do so much more quickly. The extensive focused instruction we're calling for transforms a "So what?" written in the margin from a snotty remark to shorthand for something like "Remember all of the work we did on warranting data? You have to make sure you link your data to your claim. You didn't do so here."

Two, it authorizes and prepares other students as expert respondents. That is, because you can be confident that your students are applying the same criteria as you will be and that they have had adequate practice articulating and meeting those criteria, their responses are more likely to get at what's crucial than they otherwise would have been. (More on this later.)

In the second place, doing the kind of composing to practice that we've called for throughout the book gives you and peer respondents many more opportunities for commenting on students' work than does collecting a very occasional final draft. Looking over a student's shoulder and saying, "Could anyone take a different position? Do a PMI?" or "Those data seem safe [or unsafe] to me" or "So what?" or "Nice connection" or "Remember what your audience might say in response" is more effective instruction than a comment on a paper because it can be put to immediate use.

Finally, the kind of extensive and focused instruction that we're calling for means that students' papers will be better than they otherwise would have been. The research syntheses we report in Chapter 3 make this absolutely clear. It's far less time consuming (and far more pleasurable) to respond to success than to problems.

We know with certainty that effective instruction can improve students' writing. In contrast to the dramatic positive effects of helping students develop procedural knowledge of form and substance consider what Hillocks (1986a) has to say about feedback: "Traditions in the teaching of English hold that compositions must be marked and commented upon—the more thoroughly the better. But research reported in this review suggests that such feedback has very little effect on enhancing the quality of student writing—regardless of frequency and thoroughness" (239). A simple lesson here: If you're spending the majority of your out-of-school time responding to students' papers, you're messing up. You need to spend the majority of that time planning instruction instead.

We do know, however, that grading and grades are a fact of life in schools, so we'll share some ideas about how we approached it once students had moved beyond composing to practice. We typically have had students work in writing groups of three to four. Before we ask students to work together in those groups, we discussed what makes a response useful and shared heuristics like the P-Q-P (or P-Q-S) protocol. In that protocol respondents begin by saying what they like about a work (Praise). They then share any wonderings they have about the content, form, and process of composing (Questions). Only then do they provide suggestions for improving (Polish/Suggestions).

➤ *Lesson idea*

We also work with students to employ the same grading criteria we will use through the use of analytic scales. When Michael taught high school, he and his colleagues developed a set of analytic scales that they used to grade all of their students' arguments. Figure 9.1 shows three that they used, slightly revised so they are consistent with the terms we've employed in this book.

After the preliminary instruction we detailed in Chapter 5, Michael and his colleagues gave students practice using these scales by rating a number of sample arguments written by students in previous years. Although students' ratings were remarkably consistent, class discussions focused on exploring differences of opinion. Then students worked in groups to rewrite the argument that received the lowest rating to move it up the scale.

➤ *Lesson idea*

With that preparation, students used the scales as part of their response in their peer response groups. Writers collected the scales from their group-mates and used them to inform their revisions. In addition to the final draft, Michael collected the scales that students had filled out along with a memo that briefly explained how the writer chose to respond to the feedback. Michael ultimately gave every student two scores on each assignment: one, a total of the scales points Michael had given the student's own paper, and the second, the average score the other members of the group received on their papers. Groups, as a whole, were held responsible for how each individual in the group did. You might also choose to work with your students to develop a scale for reflection and use it to assess students' memos.

As an alternative, students could rank the sample compositions. In the discussion in which students explained and justified their rankings, they would have to articulate the criteria they employed. You could track those criteria on a flip chart or interactive whiteboard and then use them to develop class-specific analytic scales. Doing so has the advantage of making certain that students have a stake in and understanding of the grading criteria. But it comes at the cost of having common assessments that can be the basis of generative collegial collaboration.

➤ *Lesson idea*

Large-Scale Assessments

Of course, we need to be mindful not only of the evaluation we do in our classrooms but also of the large-scale evaluations our students will experience. Large-scale assessments are a fact of life for all public school teachers. And as

Figure 9.1   Analytic Scales

VALIDITY

5. The writer consistently uses all elements of logical argument to persuade the reader. (See checklist.)

4. The writer fully develops at least one argument and uses only relevant data throughout the paper. The writer could improve the paper by completing undeveloped arguments or by fully developing additional one(s).

3. The writer clearly states a claim and uses some support, but that support is not effective because of a consistent problem with one element or problems with two elements.

2. The writer does not present a clear claim or consistently neglects several elements of logical argument.

1. The writer uses virtually no support.

Checklist

_____ Clear claim that's worth arguing

_____ Sufficient relevant data that provide a safe starting point

_____ Clear connection between data and claim (warrant)

Figure 9.1 *continued*

AUDIENCE

5. The writer significantly enhances the argument by appealing to the audience in more than one way.

4. The writer enhances argument by appealing to the audience.

3. The writer adjusts the argument for the audience, but the adjustment does not enhance the argument.

2. The writer does not adjust the argument for the audience.

1. The writer makes choices that will alienate the audience.

FORM

5. The writer consistently makes both organizational and stylistic choices that contribute significantly to achieving his/her purpose.

4. The writer makes both organizational and stylistic choices that contribute to achieving his/her purpose.

3. The writer makes either organizational or stylistic choices that contribute to achieving his/her purpose.

2. The writers organizational or stylistic choices are not likely to contribute to achieving his/her purpose.

1. The writers organizational and stylistic choices are not likely to contribute to achieving his/her purpose.

George Hillocks (2002) has so powerfully demonstrated, many of those assessments reward banal and formulaic writing. But, to coin a phrase, the times, they are a changing.

Fueled by Race to the Top funding the Smarter Balanced Assessment Consortium and the Partnership for Assessment of Readiness for College and Careers are developing new assessments, ones that are much more challenging. The assessments are under development so we have worked on reviewing performance task sample items on both tests. The assessments have not yet been piloted with students and they will not be in place until 2014–2015, but the draft documents give a sense of what the assessments will probably look like.

Here are two assessment tasks detailed in the Smarter Balanced Assessment Consortium draft document of September 19, 2011, that relate to writing anchor standards 7–9:

> Conduct short as well as more sustained research projects based on focused questions, demonstrating understanding of the subject under investigation; Gather relevant information from multiple print and digital sources, assess the credibility and accuracy of each source, and integrate the information while avoiding plagiarism; Draw evidence from literary or informational texts to support analysis, reflection, and research:
>
> - At middle school, students might collaboratively generate and explore a variety of potential digital and print resources that can be used to respond to a research question or problem presented. Collaborative discussions would include considering the credibility of sources located and relevance of information to the topic. Individually, students prepare and present their results to show that they can draw conclusions that integrate or analyze information (using data and/ or text evidence as support).
>
> - Using a document/media library provided, high school students might collaboratively discuss texts read and speeches or media messages viewed that present different points of view about an issue from a period in history (e.g.,

World War I, Civil Rights era). Individually, students may be asked to select appropriate sources, and then analyze and present information (academic writing/explanation) or critique perspectives/potential biases as they relate to the issue and craft a response (critique or argument). Student responses will demonstrate the ability to analyze and synthesize information, as well as evaluate sources used (primary, secondary, media, etc.) for credibility, bias, quality of evidence, and/or quality of reasoning.

These summaries give a sense of the complexity of what students will be asked to do. Sample items that we've seen provide additional detail. For example, one asked students to imagine themselves as editors of an anthology for eleventh–twelfth graders and to select three to five texts (literary and nonliterary; print and nonprint) that speak to the theme of the American dream. Among the things that the sample item asked students to do are the following:

1. Identify and analyze the perspective of those texts.
2. Compare and contrast the position that the texts take on the American Dream.
3. Evaluate the perspectives of the texts as a way to convey their own perspective.

The task requires students to put different kinds of texts into meaningful conversation. It requires them to take a principled position. It requires them to make both analytic and evaluative arguments, mining the texts as sources of data to do so.

We understand that the new assessments aren't a done deal and that there are treacherous political waters yet to be navigated, but we want to ask a simple question: Are you preparing your kids to succeed on this kind of assessment? If your answer is no, then you have to change along with the times. This need for change is clear regardless of what the next generation of tests looks like because it's clear that the kind of critical and creative thinking already required by colleges, careers, and citizenship in the twenty-first century is not tapped in most current assessments. We hope that the ideas that we've shared in this book will help you make the changes necessary to help your students meet these new challenges.

Embracing the Challenge

We began this book by arguing that we think that the CCSS can be used as a lever for progressive practice. We understand why there may be some reluctance to embrace such an argument. After all, it seems pretty clear that standards and the assessments that are designed to measure them have had a negative effect on the lives of too many teachers.

Nonetheless, we're optimistic that things will be different this time. We don't see any way that the CCSS can be met in classrooms that aren't rich with talk, with a variety of reading, and without the opportunity to develop all five kinds of knowledge through all five kinds of composing. We don't see any way the CCSS can be met in schools that aren't rich in opportunities for collaboration and professional development. In short, it seems to us that the CCSS point to what we see as best practice. In fact, we don't suggest a single instructional idea in this book that we would not have suggested were there no standards of any sort.

Carpe diem.

If we seize the day, we'll create rich unit contexts that put literary, nonliterary, and popular cultural texts into meaningful conversation. If we seize the day, we'll provide our students with the practice they need to be successful rather than with remediation after they've failed. If we seize the day, we won't read paper after paper that makes essentially the same uninteresting points but will instead read papers that are part of a vibrant, ongoing exchange. If we seize the day, we won't spend our out-of-school time trying to avoid grading the stack of papers accumulating on our desks but will instead be using that time to develop more new and creative lessons that ultimately result in students' transferring their knowledge to new reading and writing situations.

Just imagine working with your colleagues across disciplines and grade levels (since the standards are vertically aligned) to identify the arguments they make in their disciplines so that you can make connections between the literary arguments your students are crafting and their two-columns proofs, or lab reports, or the arguments they are making in their history classes about when revolution is justified, or the work they are doing in health classes on reducing alcohol or drug abuse. Just imagine their supporting your work by employing the same heuristics you do to prompt students to develop data, make connections, and anticipate and respond to the arguments of others and perhaps even by using the same analytic scales you use.

Just imagine students leaving your class continuing the conversation in which the class was engaged as they walk through the halls. Just imagine the feeling of pride even your struggling students will feel when they make public an argument you and their classmates have helped them to craft.

We don't think the imaginings we just asked of you are pipe dreams. We've experienced them ourselves. But we know they are not easy to achieve. In fact, we realize that bringing them into reality may take some significant changes.

The Five Kinds of Knowledge

One significant change that will have to occur is a re-orientation about the kind of knowledge that's most important. As we've argued throughout this book, declarative knowledge has been privileged in school. Instruction that privileges declarative knowledge of substance focuses on definitions of vocabulary word or literary terms, on the details of the texts students read, on the characteristics of genre or literary periods, or on the particulars of authors' lives or of the historical epochs in which their works are set. One indication of the prevalence of an emphasis on declarative knowledge is Applebee and Langer's (2006) finding that "many students are not writing a great deal for any of their academic subjects, including English, and most are not writing at any length" (ii). No need for extensive or extended writing. Declarative knowledge of substance can be assessed through short answer responses to texts or worksheets or fill-in-the-blank tests or multiple-choice tests.

Declarative knowledge of form most often appears in instruction in grammar or in citation format. Here's a thought experiment: think of your school system. When does instruction in grammar begin? Our guess is fifth or sixth grade, at the latest. Now when does it end? In our experience? never. That is, in school after school with which we've worked the seventh-grade teachers teach the same terms and conventions that the sixth-grade teachers do and they do so in much the same way. And the eighth. And the ninth. And tenth, eleventh, and twelfth to boot. The status quo just isn't working. Even if students gain declarative knowledge they don't learn how to put it to use.

That's why we so strongly suggest increasing our emphasis on procedural knowledge of both form and substance. We need to teach our students how to articulate claims that are clear and worth defending, how to develop sufficient relevant data, how to connect those data to those claims with warrants, and how to anticipate and respond to their audience's needs. We need to help them be able to write clear and compelling sentences and to organize their arguments so that they have the greatest possible impact. And if we focus on the *how*, students will, as a matter of course, come to understand the *what* as well.

That's also why we so strongly suggest increasing our emphasis on knowledge of context, on creating real-world contexts in which what they are learning really matters and in which students can write for real purposes. The context determines what knowledge of substance matters. It determines the kind of composing we ought to do and the form that composing should take. It determines what procedures we ought to employ in what ways. We can't be the only audience for our students and we can't focus only on the discipline of English if we are to help our students develop this knowledge. They have to write with and against texts from other disciplines to us, to their classmates, and to others as well.

The Five Kinds of Composing

If we want to realize our imaginings, we have to do more than focus on our students' final drafts. We have to provide plenty of practice so they can develop the complex skills we are trying to teach. We have to help them learn various ways of composing to plan, both so they can mine the work of others and so they can generate the stuff about which they will write. We have to give them enough new starts that they can get over the fear of the blank page and have them reflect on various ways of getting started in their first-draft writing. We have to develop clear criteria of achievement and have them work with their classmates to achieve them, both in the drafting and their revision.

And we can't be content with their final drafts, no matter how good they are. The truth is that no composition on which we work with our students, with the possible exception of their college application essays, really matters. What matters is that they can transfer what they have learned to new composing in new composing situations.

We hope that you have found the five kinds of knowledge and the five kinds of composing to be useful heuristics for examining your practice. We hope that we have presented you with enough examples of how you might employ those heuristics that you have a good idea of the kind of work you want to do with your kids to meet and even exceed the CCSS. We hope that you leave this book with the resolve to make the changes you need to make to prepare your students for college, for the world of work, and for their lives as citizens in a democracy.

Seize the day. If not now, when?

Appendix

UNIT EXAMPLE

Unit Title: American Identities and the American Dream

Unit Description (Overview Narrative): This is an introductory unit done at the beginning of a junior English class focused on American literature. Through the first several weeks of school, students establish a learning community through activities related to American identities as well as begin to address the course essential question: What is the American dream, and to what extent is it achievable for everyone? Activities range from creative writing to rhetorical analysis and culminate in writing an argument-based "This I Believe" essay about a debatable issue, using evidentiary reasoning.

The focus on argumentation throughout this unit is sometimes direct and sometimes more indirect and subtle. Students examine how an argument might be expressed through poetry and pictures. Students will be asked to examine and wonder about details in pictures that show various American experiences and ultimately take a stance on what is happening or what the purpose is of the picture's construction, or what the story behind the picture is. They will do the same with the reading and composing of poetry. The unit will culminate with both a direct argument of judgment about an issue of the American experience and identity, and a more subtle argument using persuasive writing techniques to establish their beliefs about America and the American experience and identity in their "This I Believe" essays. In this final essay, while not overtly convincing someone to agree with them, students are using persuasive **techniques to establish a valid argument about their beliefs and using support for their claims.**

Course Essential Question: What is the American dream, and to what extent is it achievable for everyone?

Unit essential question: What is an American?

Unit guiding questions:

- How do we identify and define ourselves?
- How do others identify and define us?
- How do individuals develop values and beliefs?
- How do we shape and express our identities?
- How do we shape and express our beliefs?
- In what ways have aspects of America been depicted in art and photography? How are these artistic expressions shaped by cultural values and how do they shape cultural values?
- Can art be a true depiction of our society? Is it a definitive or questionable representation?
- How have poets explored the American experience and what have they expressed about it?

Grade(s)/Level:	11
Discipline:	English/Language Arts
Course:	American Literature
Author(s):	Brandon Bolyard, Cecilia Pattee
Contact Information:	brandon.bolyard@gmail.com, cecilia.pattee@gmail.com

SECTION 1: ASSESSMENT

A. Summative Writing Assessment

Background:

Students will have studied several different aspects of how people define or establish American identities. By the end of the unit, students will have examined and written poems and analyzed several different essays about American values, experience, and identity including a few "This I Believe" essays that show a writer's beliefs in what it means to be an American or that show some aspect of traits commonly associated with American beliefs. Students will use the background from their own writing and others to write their own direct argument of judgment about American identity and their own more subtle "This I Believe" essay that will express a personal belief about American identity and values, using subtle persuasive techniques and evidentiary reasoning.

Prompt (Including Essential Question):

Using previous brainstorming from the quilt project, examination of America in pictures, and analysis of arguments of judgment and "This I Believe" essays, students write an argument of judgment using criteria developed in class, and a "This I Believe" essay to show what they believe about a core belief about America or living in America. Students use the guidelines for a "This I Believe" essay given at the program's website: http://thisibelieve.org/guidelines/.

B. Formative Assessments

Time and Prompts:

Class discussion, daily work, and creative assignments work as formative assessments. Students will engage in evidence extract activities, warrant workouts, P-M-I claim activities and debates to develop and demonstrate facility with the crux moves of argument of judgment. Students hand-draw/create quilt squares to represent identities and write informal essays arguing for the significance of the symbols they included. Students also write poems that explore and express subtle arguments about American identity and beliefs.

Starting in the third week of the unit, students begin to examine "This I Believe" essays. The examination follows an "I do. We do. You do" model for the gradual release of responsibility in which students begin to understand the components of the "This I Believe" essay as a form of argument. Examination takes the form of a PAPA square analysis in which students identify persona, audience, purpose, and audience.

SECTION 2: THE INSTRUCTIONAL LADDER

5 Kinds of Knowledge	Instructional Strategies	Common Core State Standards	See Page
On which of the 5 kinds of knowledge does the lesson focus?	*What strategies and what sequence will apprentice students to the summative writing tasks?*	*When and through which strategies are the Common Core State Standards being taught?*	*Where in this book can one read more about a specific strategy?*
	Week 1		
Knowledge of Purpose Students understand purpose of the unit, which is to examine American ideologies and establish beliefs about America. Students also understand how these beginning activities establish the collab-orative community in the classroom and how the individual identities come together to form the classroom community.	Done at the beginning of the school year, students examine the ways they define themselves and also the character traits we might associate with being American. This is a way for students to begin examining the essential question "What is an American?" 1. Students read or listen to the essay "Little Boxes" by Anthony Wright (www.facinghistory.org/little-boxes) and discuss the ways people might be categorized. Discussion focuses on the challenges of oversimplifying the ways we define ourselves. Students then create an identity map, which is used as a brainstorming activity for the Century Quilt assignment. (CCSS reading anchor standard 1)	 CCSS reading anchor standard 1 CCSS speaking and listening anchor standard 1	Four Approaches to Developing Essential Questions: pp. 39–40 (We used the first approach for this unit.) Importance of Frontloading in Inquiry Units: Ch. 4, pp. 10–12
	2. Students read the poem "Century Quilt" by Marilyn Nelson Waniek and complete an "I See/I Think/I Wonder" chart. The activity engages students in close reading of a poem and also focuses on the connota-tion of a quilt as a patchwork of different patterns. Students are guided to the idea of America being a patchwork of diversity via a Jesse Jackson quote ("America is not like a blanket-one piece of unbroken cloth, the same color, the same texture, the same size. America is more like a quilt—many patches, many pieces, many colors, many sizes, all woven and held together by a common thread").	CCSS reading anchor standards 2, 3, 6 CCSS writing anchor standard 2 CCSS speaking and listening anchor standard 1 CCSS language anchor standard 2	Analyzing/Discussing Poem and Connotation: Selecting Most Important Word with Think-Alouds: p. 81

5 Kinds of Knowledge	Instructional Strategies	Common Core State Standards	See Page
	3. Students use the identity charts and in class brainstorming to create a quilt square that represents their identities. The class decides on three things all squares must have (e.g., name, birthday, nickname, favorite color or quote, etc.). Squares are drawn/colored rather than students creating real quilt squares. Some students elect to draw simple squares, while others are more elaborate with pictures, construction paper, etc. These squares are presented to the class and the class collaborates to put the class quilt together. (Students also write an informal essay explaining the symbols/objects on the chart.)	CCSS reading anchor standards 2, 3, 6 CCSS writing standard 2 CCSS speaking and listening standard 1 CCSS language standard 2	
Week 2			
Knowledge of Purpose and Context Procedural Knowledge of Substance and Form Declarative Knowledge of Substance and Form	1. The first activity asks students to remember recent arguments and to list the reasons they have engaged in such arguments, which will be put on an anchor chart to record the purposes and contexts for arguments in our lives. This chart will be expanded as we look at the contexts and purposes for the arguments we will read through the week. Students will be asked to cite the moves and strategies that have helped them to win arguments, or conversely, that have weakened their arguments—these will be identified as elements of claims, data, warranting, and backing/reasoning about data in ways that connect the data to the claim, set rules, and reason about data, reservations, and responses to reservations. Students will get an overview of Toulminian logic and the structure of argument used in the disciplines and by the CCSS.	CCSS reading anchor standards 1–10 CCSS writing anchor standards 1, 4–6	Chapter 2, pp. 48–51
Procedural Knowledge of Form Procedural Knowledge of Substance	2. Students will be introduced to the P-M-I heuristic for claim writing and will apply this heuristic to claims like "All cars should be yellow" and "Teachers should wear mood indicators" to which students will not have prior allegiance, and then begin applying the PMI to claims about the American character:	CCSS writing anchor standard 1 CCSS speaking and listening anchor standard 1	Chapter 5, "Claims," pp. 10–13

5 Kinds of Knowledge	Instructional Strategies	Common Core State Standards	See Page
	"Americans are essentially Puritanical in attitude due to the influence of our country's original settling." Students will then generate their own claims and apply the PMI.		
	3. Students will engage in an evidence extract activity around the claim: Elvis was the greatest singer in history and football is the most American of all sports, ranking and critiquing the evidence provided, and then expressing different warrants for each. An anchor chart about valid evidence and another expressing the qualities of good reasoning (warrants and backing) will be generated. Students will then read excerpts from the argument "American Moral Exceptionalism" www.socialjudgments.com/docs/AME%20CHAPTER.POSTING.pdf with the claim: Much of American culture's unique quality stems from its Puritan-Protestant heritage and extract evidence for the claim/s and cite and evaluate the reasoning provided based on their charts.	CCSS reading anchor standards 1, 2, 7, 8 CCSS writing anchor standard 9 CCSS speaking and listening anchor standards 1–2	Generating Data, pp. 61–62
	Week 3		
Declarative Knowledge of Substance	1. Students will read "Japanese Values vs. American Values" (www.bookrags.com/essay-2005/3/22/211013/858) and discuss it in small groups. Students will read "Differences Between Japanese and American Schools" (www.difference-between.net/miscellaneous/difference-between-american-and-japanese-schools/) and work in small groups to map the differences in schools onto the differences in values. Students will be assigned a role for a simulation debate: American school administrators, teachers, parents, and students. For homework, students will research from their assigned perspective the impact of increasing the length of the American school year by 33% to bring its length in line with the length of the Japanese school year.	CCSS reading anchor standards 1, 2, 7, 8 CCSS writing anchor standard 9 CCSS speaking and listening anchor standards 1–2	

5 Kinds of Knowledge	Instructional Strategies	Common Core State Standards	See Page
Procedural Knowledge of Form and Substance	2. Debate "The American school year should be increased by 33%." Students with like roles will have one day to develop a claim, evidence, and reasoning for their position. Each group will have five minutes to present their case, receiving 5 points for a claim that meets the PMI, 3 points for each data point meeting our criteria, and 5 points for reasoning that meets our criteria. Points can be won from other teams by expressing reservations, and won back by response to reservation. Whole-class discussion on what arguments were most effective and why.	CCSS speaking and listening anchor standards 1–4, 6	Chapter 6
Declarative Knowledge of Form	3. For homework, each student will find an argument of judgment from the Internet and write a short argument about why it is an argument of judgment, both the article and responding argument to be posted on the class wiki. Next day students will do jigsaw reading and evaluating the essays.	CCSS reading anchor standards 1, 2, 5, 6 CCSS writing anchor standard 9 CCSS speaking and listening anchor standards 1–2	
Procedural Knowledge of Form and Substance	4. Students will write a short argument of judgment about what is most essential to American identity. They will work on their drafts in class and engage in peer response using the P-Q-P model and then will revise their essays.	CCSS writing anchor standards 1, 9 CCSS speaking and listening anchor standards 1–2 CCSS language anchor standards 1–3	p. 126
	Week 4		
Procedural Knowledge of Form and Substance Declarative Knowledge of Form and Substance	1. The first activity engages students in picking a picture that depicts a historical moment, landmark, geographic location, or other scene depicting America. Students complete an I See/I Wonder/ Powerful words chart. After compiling a list of the powerful words, students can see the diverse ways American experiences might be described. Students then write a poem about the picture that implicitly explores what is represented about American experience, values, and identity through the picture.	CCSS reading anchor standards 1, 2, 7, 9 CCSS writing anchor standard 4 CCSS language anchor standard 5	Procedural Knowledge of Substance: p. 23 Different Positions on the Essential Question: p. 39 Analyzing Visual Texts: pp. 83–86 Encouraging Multiple Interpretations: pp. 79–80

5 Kinds of Knowledge	Instructional Strategies	Common Core State Standards	See Page
Procedural Knowledge of Form and Substance	2. For the poetry jigsaw, students work in groups to examine a poem or song that has a connection to American identity and values. Students do some analysis of the poem and then teach the poem to other students. Poems could include "I Hear American Singing" by Walt Whitman, "The Star-Spangled Banner" by Francis Scott Key, "America the Beautiful" by Katharine Lee Bates, "Mother to Son" by Langston Hughes, and "My Country 'Tis of Thee" by Samuel Francis Smith. Students will be asked to find their own songs and poems exploring American values and identity. They will write a short argument of judgment about how the poem expresses a point, provides a pattern of evidence and reasoning in support of that point, whether explicit or implicit, transferring what they learned the previous week.	CCSS reading anchor standards 1, 2, 4, 6, 9; speaking and listening anchor standard 1	
	Week 5		
Declarative Knowledge of Form Procedural Knowledge of Substance	Students begin reading "This I Believe" essays in which writers have expressed their beliefs in America. The week follows the "I do, we do, you do" model of instruction.	CCSS reading anchor standards 1, 2, 3, 4, 6, 7, 8, 9 CCSS writing anchor standards 9 and 10 CCSS speaking and listening anchor standard 1 These standards are all repeated in each of the activities in week 5.	
	1. Students read "The Right to be Fully American" by Yasir Billoo, which is about religious freedoms and list ideas that stand out. The teacher shows students the PAPA square analysis template (Persona, Audience, Purpose, Argument)[1] and model with a think-aloud for analyzing the essay.		Procedural Knowledge of Form: p. 23 Think-Aloud Strategy: p. 31 Declarative Knowledge of Form: p. 22

5 Kinds of Knowledge	Instructional Strategies	Common Core State Standards	See Page
Procedural Knowledge of Form	2. Students then read "Tomorrow Will Be a Better Day" by Josh Rittenberger and do a PAPA square with a partner to practice the analysis process. 3. Students finish this part of the unit with reading "Life, Liberty, and the Pursuit of Happiness" by Andrew Sullivan and complete an individual PAPA square. The three essays help students understand the structure of this type of essay and give them three models of how to write a "This I Believe" essay about a belief in America.[2] 4. Students work on sentence combining activities to help them craft "This I Believe" statements.		Composing to Practice/Plan: pp. 29–32 Composing to Transfer: pp. 33–35
	Week 6		
Procedural Knowledge of Form and Substance	1. Students use the writing process to write their own "This I Believe" essay. Students brainstorm and draft essays and use a peer-editing tool by Smith and Wilhelm (2007). Students have the opportunity to share essays with the class. Discussion of students' beliefs serve as a transition to discussing the American dream and beginning the process of defining the American dream, which is the focus of the rest of the semester.	CCSS writing anchor standards 1, 3, 4, 5, 9 CCSS speaking and listening anchor standard 4 CCSS language anchor standards 1, 2, 3, 5	Declarative Knowledge of Substance: p. 22 Narrative as Argument: p. 17 First Draft Composing: p. 32 Final Draft Composing: pp. 32–33

Credit/Thanks:

Picture/Poetry activity: Diane Williams, Anser Charter School, Boise, ID

"Little Boxes" and Identity Maps/Quilt Idea: Kellie Hannum, Skyview High School, Nampa, ID

Thinking Partners/Collaborators: Christina Cochran and Scott Moore, Vallivue High School, Caldwell, ID

---

[1] PAPA analysis modified from Maxine Hairston's text Contemporary Composition (short edition)

[2] These essays come from the print edition of This I Believe (2006), but many essays can be found on the program's website http://thisibelieve.org.

Works Cited

Andrews, R. 2009. *The Importance of Argument in Education*. London: Institute of Education, University of London.

Andrews, R., C. Torgerson, G. Low, and N. McGuinn. 2009. "Teaching Argument Writing to 7- to 14-Year-Olds: An International Review of the Evidence of Successful Practice." *Cambridge Journal of Education* 39: 291–310.

Applebee, A. N., and J. Langer. 2006. "The State of Writing in American Schools: What Existing Data Tell Us." Albany, NY: Center on English Learning and Achievement.

Applebee, A. N., J. A. Langer, M. Nystrand, and A. Gamoran. 2003. "Discussion-Based Approaches to Developing Understanding: Classroom Instruction and Student Performance in Middle and High School English." *American Educational Research Journal* 40: 685–730.

Appleman, D. 2009. *Critical Encounters in High School English*, 2d ed. New York: Teachers College Press.

Beach, R. 2011. "Issues in Analyzing Alignment of Language Arts Common Core Standards with State Standards." *Educational Researcher* 40: 179–82.

Bereiter, C. 2004. "Reflections on Depth." In *Teaching for Deep Understanding*, edited by K. Leithwood, P. McAdie, N. Bascia, and A. Rodriguez, 8–12. Toronto: Elementary Teachers' Federation of Ontario (EFTO).

Booth, W. 1988. *The Company We Keep*. Berkeley: University of California Press.

Brooks, D. 2011. "If It Feels Right. . . ." *The New York Times*, September 12. Available at www.nytimes.com/2011/09/13/opinion/if-it-feels-right.html?_r=2&ref=davidbrooks, retrieved 9/23/2011.

Burke, K. [1941] 1973. *The Philosophy of Literary Form*, 3d ed. Berkeley: University of California Press.

Center for K–12 Assessment and Performance Management, ETS. 2011. "Coming Together to Raise Achievement: New Assessments for the Common Core State Standards." Available at http://k-12center.com/rsc/pdf/Assessments_for_the_Common_Core_Standards.pdf, retrieved 1/3/2012.

CNN.com. 2004. "Two French journalists kidnapped in Iraq." *CNN World*, 28 August. Available at http://articles.cnn.com/2004-08-28/world/iraq.main_1_sadr-city-al-jazeera-iraqi-police?_s=PM:WORLD, retrieved 7/11/2011.

Coles, R. 1989. *The Call of Stories: Teaching and the Moral Imagination*. Boston: Houghton Mifflin.

Conley, D. 2010. *College and Career Ready: Helping All Students Succeed Beyond High School*. San Francisco: Jossey-Bass.

Council of Chief State School Officers (CCSSO), and the National Governors Association Center for Best Practices. 2010. *Common Core State Standards for English Language Arts and Literacy in History/Social Studies, Science, and Technical Subjects, Appendix A: Research Supporting Key Elements of the Standards, Glossary of Key Terms*. Available at www.corestandards.org/assets/Appendix_A.pdf, retrieved 5/19/2011.

Council of Writing Program Administrators, the National Council of Teachers of English, and the National Writing Project. 2011. *Framework for Success in Post-Secondary Writing*. Available at http://wpacouncil.org/files/framework-for-success-postsecondary-writing.pdf, retrieved 5/9/2012.

Crowhurst, M. 1990. "Teaching and Learning the Writing of Persuasive/Argumentative Discourse." *Canadian Journal of Education* 15: 348–59.

Cunningham, M., and D. Swanson. 2010. "Educational Resilience in African American Adolescents." *Journal of Negro Education* 79: 473–87.

Cushman, E., S. Barbier, C. Mazak, and R. Petrone. 2006. "Family and Community Literacies." In *Research on Composition: Multiple Perspectives on Two Decades of Change*, edited by P. Smagorinsky. New York: Teachers College Press.

Dubner, S. J., and S. D. Levitt. 2006. "A Star Is Made." *The New York Times Magazine*, 7 May. Available at www.nytimes.com/2006/05/07/magazine/07wwln_freak.html?pagewanted=al, retrieved 7/7/2011.

Fredricksen, J., J. D. Wilhelm, and M. W. Smith. 2012. *So, What's the Story? Teaching Narrative to Understand Ourselves, Others, and the World*. Portsmouth, NH: Heinemann.

Gladwell, M. 2009. "The Courthouse Ring: Atticus Finch and the Limits of Southern Liberalism." *The New Yorker* (August 10). Available at www.newyorker.com/reporting/2009/08/10/090810fa_fact_gladwell, retrieved 8/13/2009.

Gocsik, Karen. 2005. "What Is an Academic Paper?" on Dartmouth College's Writing Program webpage. Available at www.dartmouth.edu/~writing/materials/student/ac_paper/what.shtml, retrieved 3/13/2012.

Graesser, A. C., D. S. McNamara, and J. Kulikowich. 2011. "Coh-Metrix: Providing Multilevel Analyses of Text Characteristics." *Educational Researcher* 40: 223–34.

Graff, G., and C. Birkenstein. 2010. *They Say/I Say: The Moves That Matter in Academic Writing*. New York: W.W. Norton.

Graham, S., and D. Perin. 2007. *Writing Next: Effective Strategies to Improve Writing of Adolescents in Middle and High Schools*. A Report to the Carnegie Corporation of New York. Washington, DC: Alliance for Excellent Education.

Greene, S. 1992. "Mining Texts in Reading to Write." *Journal of Advanced Composition* 12: 151–70.

Halstead, D. n.d. "The Writers Challenge: Credibility, Argument, and Structure in Public Health Writing." Available at www.hsph.harvard.edu/studentlife /orientation/files/Halstead_Writers_Challenge.pdf, retrieved 5/19/2011.

Haskell, R. 2001. *Transfer of Learning: Cognition, Instruction, and Reasoning*. San Diego: Academic Press.

Hillocks, G. Jr. 1986a. *Research on Written Composition: New Directions for Teaching*. Urbana, IL: ERIC and National Conference for Research in English.

———. 1986b. "The Writer's Knowledge: Theory, Research, and Implications for Practice." In *The Teaching of Writing* (85th Yearbook of the National Society for the Study of Education, Part 2), edited by A. Petrosky and D. Bartholomae, 71–94. Chicago: National Society for the Study of Education.

———. 1995. *Teaching Writing as Reflective Practice*. New York: Teachers College Press.

———. 2002. *The Testing Trap: How State Writing Assessments Control Learning*. New York: Teachers College Press.

———. 2011. *Teaching Argument Writing, Grades 6–12*. Portsmouth, NH: Heinemann.

Hillocks, G., B. McCabe, and J. McCampbell. 1971. *The Dynamics of English Instruction, Grades 7–12*. New York: Random House.

Hull, G., and K. Schultz, eds. 2002. *School's Out: Bridging Out-of-School Literacies with Classroom Practice*. New York: Teachers College Press.

Ingram, I. 2011. "Fear of a Blank Page." Available at www.ianingram.com/blog /fear-of-a-blank-page/, retrieved 7/5/2011.

Johannessen, L. R., E. A. Kahn, and C. C. Walter. 2009. *Writing About Literature*, 2d ed. Urbana, IL: National Council of Teachers of English.

Johnson, S., and B. Howard. 2000. "Young Adolescents Displaying Resilient and Non-Resilient Behaviour: Insights from a Qualitative Study—Can Schools Make a Difference?" Available at http://trove.nla.gov.au/work/153117473, retrieved 5/8/2012.

Keith, W., and D. Beard. 2008. "Toulmin's Rhetorical Logic: What's the Warrant for Warrants?" *Philosophy and Rhetoric* 41 (1): 22–50.

Langer, J. A. 2001. "Beating the Odds: Teaching Middle and High School Students to Read and Write Well." *American Educational Research Journal* 38: 837–80.

Lunsford, K. J. 2002. "Contextualizing Toulmin's Model in the Writing Classroom: A Case Study." *Written Communication* 19: 109–74.

Lunsford, A. A., J. J. Ruszkiewicz, and K. Walters. 2007. *Everything's an Argument*. 4th ed. New York: Bedford/St. Martin's.

Mahiri, J. 2004. "New Literacies in a New Century." In *What They Don't Learn in School: Literacy in the Lives of Urban Youth*, edited by J. Mahiri, 1–19. New York: Peter Lang.

Marshall, J. D., P. Smagorinsky, and M. W. Smith. 1995. *The Language of Interpretation: Patterns of Discourse in Discussions of Literature*. Urbana, IL: NCTE.

McCann, T., L. R. Johannessen, E. Kahn, and J. Flanagan. 2006. *Talking in Class: Using Discussion to Enhance Teaching and Learning*. Urbana, IL: National Council of Teachers of English.

McCann, T., L. R. Johannessen, E. Kahn, P. Smagorinsky, and M. W. Smith, eds. 2005. *Reflective Teaching, Reflective Learning: How to Develop Critically Engaged Readers, Writers, and Speakers*. Portsmouth, NH: Heinemann.

Monahan, M. E. 2001. Raising Voices: How Sixth Graders Construct Authority and Knowledge in Argumentative Essays. Unpublished doctoral dissertation, Rutgers University, New Brunswick, NJ.

Moore, D. W., D. J. Short, M. W. Smith, and A. W. Tatum. 2007. *Hampton-Brown Edge* (Level B). Carmel, CA: National Geographic School Publishing/Hampton-Brown.

Moore, M. 2011. "Cornering the Education Market." *Savannah Morning News* (May 4). Available at http://savannahnow.com/column/2011-05-04/moore-cornering-education-market, retrieved 5/25/2011.

Newell, G., R. Beach, J. Smith, and J. VanDerHeide. 2011. "Teaching and Learning Argumentative Reading and Writing: A Review of Research." *Reading Research Quarterly* 46: 273–304.

Nickerson, R. 1985. "Understanding Understanding." *American Journal of Education* 93: 201–39.

Perkins, D. N., and G. Salomon. 1988. "Teaching for Transfer." *Educational Leadership* 46 (1): 22–32.

Porter, A., J. McMaken, J. Hwang, and R. Yang. 2011. "Common Core Standards: The New U.S. Intended Curriculum." *Educational Researcher* 40: 103–16.

Rabinowitz, P. 1987. *Before Reading: Narrative Conventions and the Politics of Interpretation.* Ithaca, NY: Cornell University Press.

Rabinowitz, P., and M. W. Smith. 1998. *Authorizing Readers: Resistance and Respect in the Teaching of Literature.* New York: Teachers College Press.

Ravitch, D. 2010. *The Death and Life of the Great American School System: How Testing and Choice Are Undermining Education.* New York: Basic Books.

Reid, A. n.d. "A Practical Guide for Writing Proposals." Available at http://facstaff .gpc.edu/~ebrown/pracguid.htm, retrieved 5/19/2011.

Reyes, J., and M. Elias. 2011. "Fostering Social-Emotional Resilience Among Latino Youth." *Psychology in the Schools* 48: 723–37.

Rex, L., and D. McEachen. 1999. "'If Anything Is Odd, Inappropriate, Confusing, or Boring, It's Probably Important': The Emergence of Inclusive Academic Literacy Through English Classroom Discussion Practices." *Research in the Teaching of English* 34 (August): 65–129.

Robb, L. 2010. *Teaching Middle School Writers: What Every English Teachers Needs to Know.* Portsmouth, NH: Heinemann.

Smagorinsky, P. 1995. "Constructing Meaning in the Disciplines: Reconceptualizing Writing Across the Curriculum as Composing Across the Curriculum." *American Journal of Education* 103: 160–84.

———. 1997. "Artistic Composing as Representational Process." *Journal of Applied Developmental Psychology* 18: 87–105.

Smagorinsky, P., V. Pettis, and P. Reed. 2004. "High School Students' Compositions of Ranch Designs: Implications for Academic and Personal Achievement." *Written Communication* 21: 386–418.

Smagorinsky, P., and M. W. Smith. 1992. "The Nature of Knowledge in Composition and Literary Understanding: The Question of Specificity." *Review of Educational Research* 62: 279–306.

Smagorinsky, P., M. Zoss, and P. Reed. 2006. "Residential Interior Design as Complex Composition: A Case Study of a High School Senior's Composing Process." *Written Communication* 23: 295–330.

Smith, M. W. 2007. "Boys and Writing." In *Teaching the Neglected "R": Rethinking Writing Instruction,* edited by R. Kent and T. Newkirk, 243–53. Portsmouth, NH: Heinemann.

Smith, M. W., and B. Connolly. 2005. "The Effects of Interpretive Authority on Classroom Discussions of Poetry: Lessons from One Teacher." *Communication Education* 54: 271–88.

Smith, M. W., and J. Wilhelm. 2002. *"Reading Don't Fix No Chevys": Literacy in the Lives of Young Men*. Portsmouth, NH: Heinemann.

———. 2006. *Going with the Flow: How to Engage Boys (and Girls) in Their Literacy Learning*. Portsmouth, NH: Heinemann.

———. 2007. *Getting It Right: Fresh Approaches to Teaching Grammar, Usage, and Correctness*. New York: Scholastic.

———. 2010. *Fresh Takes on Teaching Literary Elements: How to Teach What Really Matters About Character, Setting, Point of View, and Theme*. New York: Scholastic.

Smith, M., J. Cheville, and G. Hillocks Jr. 2006. "'I guess I'd better watch my English': Grammar and the Teaching of English Language Arts." In *Handbook on Writing Research*, edited by C. MacArthur, S. Graham, and J. Fitzgerald, 263–74. New York: Guilford Press.

Toulmin, S. 1958. *The Uses of Argument*. New York: Cambridge University Press.

Toulmin, S., R. Rieke, and A. Janik. 1984. *An Introduction to Reasoning*, 2d ed. New York: Macmillan.

Troyka, L. 1973. "A Study of the Effect of Simulation-Gaming on Expository Prose Competence of College Remedial English Composition Students." Dissertations Abstracts International, 4092-A.

Turner, K. H. 2005. Toulmin and Transfer: The Impact of Instruction in Argument on Students' Writing Across Disciplines. Unpublished doctoral dissertation, Rutgers University, New Brunswick, NJ.

Vygotsky, L. S. 1987. "Thinking and Speech." In *Collected Works*, Vol. 1 by L. S. Vygotsky, edited by R. Rieber and A. Carton, 39–285. Translated by N. Minick. New York: Plenum.

Wilhelm, J. 1997/2008. *You Gotta BE the Book: Teaching Engaged and Reflective Reading with Adolescents*. New York: Teachers College Press.

———. 2001. *Improving Comprehension with Think-Alouds*. New York: Scholastic.

———. 2002. *Action Strategies for Deepening Comprehension: Using Drama Strategies to Assist Improved Reading Performance*. New York: Scholastic.

———. 2007. *Engaging Readers and Writers with Inquiry*. New York: Scholastic.

Wilhelm, J., and B. Edmiston. 1998. *Imagining to Learn: Inquiry, Ethics and Integration Through Drama*. Portsmouth, NH: Heinemann.

Wilhelm, J. D., and B. Novak. 2011. *Teaching Literacy for Love and Wisdom: Being the Book and Being the Change*. New York: Teachers College Press.

Wilhelm, J. D., T. Baker, and J. Dube-Hackett. 2001. *Strategic Reading: Guiding Adolescents to Lifelong Literacy*. Portsmouth, NH: Heinemann.

Wilhelm, J. D., M. W. Smith, and J. E. Fredricksen. 2012. *Get It Done! Writing and Analyzing Informational Texts to Make Things Happen*. Portsmouth, NH: Heinemann.

Writing Center, University of North Carolina at Chapel Hill. 2010–2012. "Argument." Handout on UNC's Writing Center webpage. Available at http://writingcenter.unc.edu/resources/handouts-demos/writing-the-paper/argument, retrieved 3/13/2012.

Index

formal speaking opportunities, 68
introducing Toulmin model with,
    48–51
preparing for, 64–65
value of, 67
warrants in, 63–64
organization, 121–24
    correspondence concept, 123–24
    five-paragraph essays, 122–23
    importance of, 124
    of movie reviews, 122

paintings, 83–85
PARCC test, 123, 124
parlor metaphor, 99–100
Partnership for Assessment of Readiness
    for College and Careers, 130
Pattee, Cecilia, 44, 137–44
patterns, 82, 83
peer response groups, 126, 127
Perin, D., 24, 114
Perkins, D. N., 33
persuasion, 16–17
persuasive writing, 11
Petrone, R., 29
Pettis, V., 29
Phillips, Michael, 122
plagiarism, 96
planning
    composing to plan, 31–32, 34
    for simulations and debates, 72–76
    text, 24
PMI (Plus/Minus/Interesting) lessons,
    56–57, 82
poetry, 80
policies, 56. *See also* public policy issues
political discourse. *See also* public policy
    issues
    argumentation and, 3
    essential questions and, 40–41
Porter, A., 6
portraits, 85
Postman, Neil, 6

P-Q-P (P-Q-S) protocol, 126
practice
    effectiveness of, 30–31
    learning and, 20
    quantity of, 31
    simulations and debates and, 76
    talent and, 30
precision, 3–4
print ads, 51–55
problems
    engaging students with, 67–68
    formulation of, 3–4
procedural knowledge, 20–21, 23–24
    declarative knowledge and, 24
    developing, 30
    final draft composing and, 32–33
    "how" kind of knowledge, 20
    inquiry knowledge and, 45
    value of, 119
    writing instruction and, 24
procedural knowledge of form, 21
    class discussion, 48
    defined, 23
    encouraging, 134
    at genre level, 23
    inquiry unit example, 140–44
    at sentence level, 23
    sentences, 113–21
    student understanding of, 28
    at text level, 23
    using, 28, 36, 113
procedural knowledge of substance, 21
    encouraging, 81, 134
    inquiry unit example, 140–44
    student understanding of, 28
proposals, 5
public policy issues
    claims in, 79
    debates on, 69–72
    identifying for inquiry study units, 73
    identifying those affected by, 74
    organizational approaches to, 122
    resilience and, 96–97